TOUR TEMPO 2

TOUR TEMPO 2

THE SHORT GAME & BEYOND

JOHN NOVOSEL WITH JOHN GARRITY

Golf's Last Secret Further Revealed

Publisher: Tour Tempo Europe B.V.

Nieuwe Diep 40

4465AB Goes, The Netherlands

E: golf@tourtempo.eu

W: www.tourtempo.eu

Printed in The Netherlands

ISBN-978-90-819595-0-6

Contents

Foreword 1

Introduction 5

Prologue 9

PART ONE: THE SHORT GAME

1. A Rebel With Barely a Clue *19*

2. The Tempo Trials *29*

3. Putting *35*

4. Chipping and Pitching *43*

5. Sand Play *49*

6. John Novosel's Little Red Book *57*

PART TWO: TOWARD A BETTER UNDERSTANDING OF TEMPO

7. Dawn of a New Paradigm *65*

8. Real Science *71*

9. Tour Tempo: The Cliffs Notes *77*

10. We're Still Learning *83*

11. Playing by the Rules *95*

12. Tempo FAQs *101*

PART THREE: THE PRO-SPECTIVE ON TEMPO

13. Proamble *113*

14. General Observations *119*

15. Tiger Watch *125*

16. Case Studies *143*

17. Pro Tempo FAQs *153*

18. John Novosel Jr.'s Little Red Book *159*

• The Force • *169*

THE BAG ROOM

Tour Tempo Book *181*

Power Tools *183*

SpeedBall *185*

VIP Golf School *187*

Total Game App *189*

John Garrity *191*

Links *193*

Foreword
by John Novosel Jr.

I'm sure many people snickered when they read the original *Tour Tempo's* subtitle: *Golf's Last Secret Finally Revealed*. It was a pretty bold claim. Published in 2004 by Doubleday and written by my dad and *Sports Illustrated* senior writer John Garrity, *Tour Tempo* challenged the myths surrounding golf's most elusive fundamental and argued that amateur golfers could dramatically improve their ball striking—instantly, in most cases—by copying the swing rhythm of the pros.

So when the book came out, we were all excited. And when I say "all," I mean the entire Novosel family. I was Dad's principal guinea pig, his resident teaching pro, and the cover boy whose left-handed swing—superimposed on the face of a stopwatch—graced the *Tour Tempo* dust jacket. My brothers JJ and Scott, living in Japan, were also major contributors to Team Novosel. JJ, our IT director, designed the Tour Tempo Web site, edited sound and video for the *Tour Tempo* CD, and produced the songs for the *Tour Tempo Tracks* CDs, musical adaptations of the now-famous tempo training tones. Scott, a former Kansas Jayhawk basketball player and competitive long-driver turned personal trainer/motivator, worked for Tour Tempo in many roles, including instruction, video production, graphic design, and product assembly.

————

The first feedback, from golfers who bought their copies on Amazon.com, came before *Tour Tempo* had even found its way into the nation's bookstores. The online golf message boards lit up with unsolicited testimonials. "Have you read all these reviews for *Tour Tempo*?" asked a single-digit handicapper. "Guys talking about hitting the ball better than they ever have, scoring better than they ever have? Hard to believe isn't it? But I was blown away by the effectiveness of this book. This [Novosel] guy is for real." Another golfer, from Illinois, called the authors "messengers of the Golf Gods .... Your instruction not only delivers miracle results, it produces a natural high."

E-mails began pouring into TourTempo.com. One of them, from out of the blue, was from retired IMG vice president Hughes Norton, Tiger Woods's former agent. Norton said his handicap had climbed from 4 to 11 despite— "or perhaps because of"—the numerous lessons he had taken from famous pros and the tips he had gotten while playing with the likes of Woods, Mark O'Meara, Curtis Strange, and Greg Norman. "I bought your book yesterday and read it last night," Norton wrote. "Today, at my golf club in Cleveland, I hit some of the most amazing golf shots in years. Just like the testimonials in your book, the ball is going farther, straighter and with a little draw. WOW! And the most amazing thing is, THERE IS NOT ONE THOUGHT OF SWING MECHANICS! You can't properly appreciate my joy!"

Another e-mail came from Barney Adams, founder of Adams Golf, who said that publishers had sent him hundreds of instruction books over the years, but ours was the only one he had read from cover to cover. "The others," he said, "ninety percent of what they offer is the same old stuff—grip it like this, the takeaway, the shoulder turn."

Norton and Adams, it went without saying, were extremely knowledge-able about golf. But they hadn't known—couldn't have known—the truth about tempo.

The testimonials were gratifying, and we gathered even more momentum from Golf Channel's coverage of a Tour Tempo clinic at New York's Chelsea Piers Driving Range and from feature spreads in *Travel + Leisure Golf* and

Golf for Women. To meet demand, Doubleday went back to press again and again. *Tour Tempo* consistently topped Amazon's best-seller list for golf.

———

We were still waiting for the backlash. Conventional wisdom said that tempo in golf was individual and reflected a golfer's personality, but my dad insisted that tempo was the same for all good players—a 3-to-1 elapsed-time ratio of backswing to forward swing through impact. The top teaching pros taught amateurs to swing back "low and slow," but Dad had empirical data proving that pro swings were very fast. If that wasn't controversial enough, converts to Tour Tempo reported that their games improved because swinging to the tempo tones cleared their minds of the swing-key clutter and check-list confusion left by conventional instruction.

We began to hear that nationally-known teaching pros were taking the *Tour Tempo* CD to the lesson tee. Then we got the stunning news that two Yale University professors, working with the students of famed instructor David Leadbetter, had not only validated Dad's 3-to-1 tempo ratio, but had suggested that similar formulas applied to all springlike systems, from automotive shock absorbers to NFL quarterbacks' throwing arms. Further validation came from Johan Hampf, education director for the Swedish PGA, who asked us to present to the Swedish teaching pros at their annual meeting. "We tried to work with tempo for a long time," Johan told me, "but this is the first time we've found anything that works externally. In the past we used internal cues, but it wasn't as consistent. You had what we were looking for."

Best of all was the feedback from the tour players themselves. It didn't come in the form of paid endorsements. It came in the form of acceptance. Many tour players now practice or warm up to the *beep—beep-beep* of our tempo tones, and even those who don't use it employ Tour Tempo jargon, describing themselves as 24/8s or 21/7s. Our biggest thrill, by far, was watching Padraig Harrington, an early Tour Tempo adopter, win three major championships in the span of 13 months.

The Doubleday edition is now in its 11th printing; Japanese and Spanish-language editions continue to sell. But Tour Tempo has grown from a book into a brand. Our company operates the Tour Tempo VIP Golf School and markets several training tools, including the Tour Tempo Micro Player,® the

SandEasy® training wedge, the Electric Putter,™ the revolutionary SpeedBall® power-enhancing system, and Dad's latest and greatest invention, the Power Tools® clubs.

You'll find mention of the above training tools throughout the book because they are special. They're special because they allow you to learn the mechanics and tempo of a particular shot *at the same time*. Let me emphasize that you don't *have* to have them to get great results. We get testimonials every week from golfers who have improved their games with the book and tones alone. But I'm a big believer in Dad's training aids. They really work.

The Tour Tempo training tones and videos are also available as apps for the Apple iPhone and iPad and numerous other platforms, including all Android devices. And now, taking advantage of evolving technology, we've also released *Tour Tempo 2: The Short Game & Beyond* as an e-book.

We hope you like *TT2*. Or perhaps I should say, *beep ... beep-beep,* we're counting on it.

(John Novosel Jr., Director of Instruction for Tour Tempo, is a distance coach to PGA Tour and LPGA Tour pros. Despite being only 6-feet tall and 165 pounds, he achieves clubhead speeds at impact of more than 140 miles per hour and ball speeds of up to 200 mph. His longest drive in RE/MAX World Long Drive competition is 402 yards.)

Introduction
by John Garrity

John Novosel's *Tour Tempo,* published in 2004, was an instant classic. Its central argument—that tempo, the most important fundamental of the golf swing, can be learned quickly and easily without expensive lessons or exhaustive practice—is now accepted by swing coaches at every level of the game. The world's top teachers play the *Tour Tempo* CD on their lesson tees. Tournament pros on six continents work Tour Tempo training into their practice routines. Tour Tempo has even captured the attention of scientists. (See "Towards a Biomechanical Understanding of Tempo in the Golf Swing," published by Yale professors Robert D. Grober and Jacek Cholewicki.) Look up and down the tee line at your local driving range or golf club; you'll see golfers with iPod cords dangling from their ears. Trust me, they aren't listening to Lady Gaga.

But *Tour Tempo* told only half the story. John's original research focused on the full swing because, as he confesses in these pages, "I wasn't that interested in the short game. Like everyone else, I wanted to hit the long ball." A second reason was the observable fact that the touring pros did not putt, chip, or hit short pitch shots with the 3-to-1 backswing-to-downswing ratio they employed for longer shots. But now, thanks to hundreds of hours of further research by Team Novosel, John has data proving that most great golfers use a 2-to-1 ratio when they make their shorter swings. And, as was the case with full-swing tempo, this short-game timing, once mastered, cures many of the mechanical faults that plague golfers—including the dreaded "yips."

We're back, therefore, with a sequel. *Tour Tempo 2: The Short Game & Beyond.*

———

Why not simply *Tour Tempo 2: The Short Game?* Three reasons.

1. In order to practice and master short-game tempo, all you need is a chapter or two explaining the concept. Then you'll be off to the practice green with this book's *Tour Tempo 2* training tones, the *Tour Tempo Micro Player* or the *Tour Tempo: Total Game* app with video demonstrations and training tones.

2. We want to share what John Novosel and John Novosel Jr. have learned about the full swing since 2004. *Tour Tempo* de-mystified the golf swing—that's why we subtitled it *Golf's Last Secret Finally Revealed*—but it didn't satisfy some golfers' hunger for the how and why. *Tour Tempo 2* provides a deeper understanding of the underlying principles.

3. We want to dish about Tiger and Phil. Fans of *Tour Tempo* told us they found John's analysis of tour swings to be as fascinating as his instruction, and we have gotten strong reader response to his "Tiger's Tempo" reports for Golf.com and *SI Golf Plus*. It may surprise you, for instance, to learn that Phil Mickelson did not lose the 2006 U.S. Open because he was an "idiot." (Mickelson's self-diagnosis.) No, Lefty lost that tournament because his tempo deserted him down the stretch, causing him to smash his ball into tree limbs, trash bags and hospitality tents.

With these thoughts in mind, we have organized our material into sections titled "The Short Game," "Toward a Better Understanding of Tempo," and "The Pro-spective on Tempo." Each section includes a selection of reader FAQ's, and there are two chapters of "Little Red Book," in which the inventor and his oldest son bolster their data with anecdotes culled from six years as tempo consultants to golfers of all abilities.

———

To sum up, *Tour Tempo 2: The Short Game & Beyond* applies John Novosel's revolutionary tempo theory to the "scoring shots"—the putts, chips and pitches from 60 yards or less that make up the majority of strokes played in a round of golf. In addition, *TT2* serves as a master class in full-swing theory and as an insightful study of the shotmaking abilities of the game's top players.

Tour Tempo spawned imitators, but this long-awaited sequel reminds us that while tempo itself can be duplicated—and must be, if you're to play well—there is only one genuine, original, *Tour Tempo*.

Prologue

The Strange Case of Tiger Woods

Once upon a time there was a tour player so good that the other pros treated him like a god.

"You get the feeling sometimes that the rest of us are all playing for second place," said Fred Couples.

"The guy is simply in a different league," said Nick Faldo.

"I didn't win any tournaments by 15 shots," said Jack Nicklaus. "When he gets ahead, I think he's superior to me."

"You can just feel that he's better than you, and he *knows* he's better than you," said Johnny Miller.

"He's raised the bar to a level only he can reach," said Tom Watson. "Someday I'll tell my grandkids that I played in the same tournament with Tiger Woods."

The record book said pretty much the same thing. From 1999 through 2003, Tiger Woods won more than a third of the tournaments he entered, a percentage that nobody in the history of golf had even approached. As recently as 2009, his winning percentage hovered near 30%, almost ten points higher than that of Ben Hogan, the only other pro with a win rate above 20%.

Woods won often, but he also won big. He won his first major, the 1997 Masters, by a record 12 strokes. He ran away with the 2000 U.S. Open at Pebble Beach by a record 15 strokes, and a month later he won the Open Championship at St. Andrews by eight. The following spring, when he slipped on his second green jacket, he owned all four major titles at the same time. Call it the Tiger Slam, if you must, but it was the qualitative equal of golf's modern Grand Slam. On top of that, Woods won between five and nine PGA Tour events in each of those years. He was Player of the Year *every* year. He won the Vardon Trophy for low scoring average *every* year. He was the leading money winner *every* year.

And he had the best tempo.

———

By best tempo I mean most *consistent*. Virtually every tour player swings at about a 3-to-1 ratio of backswing to forward swing, so you could argue that they all have the best tempo. But tournament pros are not robots; some of their swings deviate fractionally. This is especially true at tournaments, where nervousness, variations in stance and lie, weather conditions and other variables conspire to throw off a pro's timing.

The better measure of a golfer's tempo is *repeatability*. Which tour pros can count on their inner clock to function flawlessly over four rounds of tournament golf?

The best way to answer that question is to collect video of the pros under tournament conditions and then check for variability in their swing times. "I have done this over the last two years," I wrote in *Tour Tempo*, "so I can say with reasonable certainty that the pro with the most perfect timing is (drum roll) ... Tiger Woods!"

Okay, Woods winning the 2004 "Novi" for Best Tempo was no shock. But the consistency of his timing was beyond comprehension. I studied videotape of the 2002 U.S. Open at Bethpage Black, which showed Tiger warming up for his final round and then shooting a cautious 72 to win his eighth major. When I timed his range swings, I was tempted to shake my laptop to see if it was broken. *Every single backswing timed out at 24 frames of broadcast-standard video.* Mid-length pitches, full wedges, mid-irons, long-irons, fairway-wood stingers, drives—no matter how short or long his backswing, they all got the same 24-frame windup. Could Tiger take it to the first tee? *Oh yeah.* He drilled a 3-wood down the fairway and then floated a wedge to the middle of the first green. Both shots were 24/8.

The commentators strained for metaphors to explain Tiger's consistency. They compared him to clockworks, assembly lines, computer hard drives, Iron Byron, even *pi*. "Cheering for Woods in a major," wrote *Sports Illustrated's* Michael Silver, "is like rooting for rain in a thunderstorm."

Ben Hogan, at his best, might have had a swing as repeatable as Tiger's. (I'd need more video of Hogan to check that out.) I find it interesting that both golfers achieved their preternatural consistency with *rebuilt swings*. Hogan fought a hook for years and didn't become *Hogan!* until he found his famous "secret," some undisclosed adjustment of grip and takeaway that allowed him to move the club back to the ball as fast as he wanted with no chance of putting hook spin on it. Woods, in a move that shocked observers at the time, simply scrapped the swing he used to win the '97 Masters and started building a new one under the supervision of swing coach Butch Harmon.

It's hard to argue retroactively against the swing change. Once Woods got the new moves down, which took the better part of a year, he went on a half-decade tear highlighted by the Tiger Slam, a six-tournament winning streak, and a whole slew of only-a-computer-would-know feats such as "first player to win five or more PGA events in five consecutive seasons." There are qualified teaching pros who can give you a before-and-after analysis of Tiger's "Harmonization," but I'm not one of them.

The only thing I can contribute to the discussion is my tempo data, which says that Woods swung *faster* in 2000 than he did in 1997. That's faster as in "elapsed time," not clubhead speed. Tiger's rebuilt swing pared thirteen-hundredths of a second off his rookie-year swing, which is the equivalent of four frames of video.

But while Woods got faster, he still maintained the critical 3-to-1 timing ratio. When I first timed him, using tape from the 1997 Masters, he was a consistent 27/9. Five years later, with eight more major titles under his belt, he was an even steadier 24/8.

Different swings, yes. But identical in their adherence to Tour Tempo.

———

Perfection must be a drag, because Tiger went rogue again. In 2002, frustrated with his progress converting from a power draw to a power fade, Woods fired Harmon and hired Dallas-based Hank Haney, swing coach to tour veteran

Mark O'Meara. Haney's prescription for Tiger's swing ailment—an ailment that only he and Tiger lost sleep over—was a faster, flatter backswing with less wrist cock. It was a less pretty swing—Tiger's head bobbed like a cork on a wave—and it delivered only one win in a season that saw Woods temporarily lose his number-one world ranking to Vijay Singh. But Woods silenced the Haney haters with a 6-win season in 2005 that included a fourth green jacket and a second claret jug. Thus began another five-year stretch of dominant play by Woods, culminating in his golfing-on-one-leg playoff victory over Rocco Mediate at the 2008 U.S. Open at Torrey Pines.

Did I say he *silenced* the Haney haters? That would be wrong. Tiger kept winning—six times in 2009 alone, despite missing two-thirds of the previous season to knee surgeries—but it was obvious that his long game was ragged. He still hit it farther than most off the tee, but young lions like Bubba Watson and Dustin Johnson sailed their tee shots 20 yards past him. More alarmingly, Woods found it increasingly difficult to find the fairway. At the 2006 Ryder Cup, he yanked his opening drive in a four-ball match into a K-Club pond that wasn't thought to be in play. "Tiger's opening tee shot made us all feel at ease," said England's Colin Montgomerie. It was a taunt that a younger Tiger had never heard.

The What's Wrong with Tiger Club was led by TV analysts Johnny Miller, Peter Kostis and Brandel Chamblee, who scribbled telestrator lines over stop-action video of the great man's swing. Tiger was hitting it wildly, echoed *GOLF Magazine's* Top 100 Teaching Pros, because he was hanging (or not hanging) on his right side through impact while coming (or not coming) out of his spine angle early instead of aggressively "sitting" into his right hamstring before exploding up into a plank-like left side, although the incredible torque produced by that move had probably damaged his left/right ankle/knee/collarbone and C2 and/or C3 vertebrae, causing him to "get stuck"—which was the problem that had led Tiger to switch coaches in the first place.

Woods dismissed his critics. He said he was "getting close."

———

It wasn't my fight. Nevertheless, I half expected the phone to ring and a vaguely familiar voice to say, "This is Hank Haney, and I was just wondering if you had any fresh tempo numbers on Tiger," or, "This is Brandel Chamblee, and

I need some evidence to support my contention that Tiger is really screwing up his swing."

I was ready for either call. I had data showing that Tiger's 2005 swing was faster than his 2002 swing (which, you'll remember, had been faster than his 1997 swing). With Harmon at the helm, Woods had been a steady 24/8. With Haney at the helm, Woods was a 21/7.

Note that I didn't say a *steady* 21/7. As he struggled to master his new swing, Tiger seemed to have turned off his internal clock. Some backswings took 22 frames, but others took 19 frames. If one forward swing clocked out at 8, the next might be a 7. Then there were the Tiger swings that seemed to have been cobbled together from different golfers—a Byron Nelson backswing, say, with a Moe Norman downswing (23/6). A Rickie Fowler takeaway leading to a Ben Hogan strike (19/7).

The variability did not surprise me. When a golfer, even a great golfer like Woods, is consciously manipulating the club, his timing will suffer. The fact that Tiger was swinging faster didn't raise any red flags, either. The so-called "Big Three" of the 1960s—Jack Nicklaus, Arnold Palmer and Gary Player—all swung at 21/7 or slightly faster. So it was only a matter of time, I told people, before Woods got comfortable with his new mechanics and regained his rhythm.

A year passed, then another, but Tiger's timing ratio refused to settle around a Tour Tempo node. His swings had a "lurchy" quality, like a man trying to heave a sack of grain onto a dock. ("I don't get why Tiger keeps trying to kill the ball," said a well-known tour pro. "He can outdrive most of us with a smooth 3-wood.") Tiger hit his best shots with a 21/7 swing, but it wasn't a tempo he could summon at will.

Why couldn't he?

It's a fair question, when you consider that our Tour Tempo CD with the training tones had by this time found its way to lesson tees around the world. Padraig Harrington, ostensibly one of Tiger's better friends on tour, added tempo training to his routine and promptly won three major champion-ships. Thousands of weekend golfers, meanwhile, practiced to the 21/7 tones on their iPods. The only two guys on the planet who didn't know that bad tempo could be corrected in five minutes were the world's greatest golfer ... and Charles Barkley.

I had to consider another possibility: that Tiger Woods was the first "post-tempo" golf star, a player so gifted that he could disregard rhythm and timing and simply *will* his ball into the hole. In 2009, after all, he won those six PGA Tour events, won all five of his Presidents Cup matches, and closed out the season with a two-stroke victory at the Australian Masters.

Anyway, it was pretty clear that Tiger wasn't going to call.

Then came that fateful Thanksgiving weekend, when Tiger crashed his car—proving that Tour Tempo was not, as we had claimed on the book jacket, "golf's last secret finally revealed."

————

Woods didn't play again until the 2010 Masters. Naturally, I was eager to see how four months away from the game, including a stint in rehab, had affected his tempo. I started by capturing some first-round video and running it through the editor in my attic studio. The first swing I timed was Tiger hitting a fairway metal from 244 yards on the par-5 eighth, a brilliant shot that stopped about eight feet from the hole.

"It was a 20/6," I told my *Tour Tempo* co-author, John Garrity, who was on the phone from the Augusta National press room. "That's pretty close. Maybe one frame off on the downswing."

"You're assuming Tiger is now a 21/7?"

"Exactly."

I took a minute to explain the implications of Tiger speeding up from 24/8 to, say, 20/7. "You take four frames out of 24, that's about a seventh of a second. And one frame on the downswing, that's three feet of clubhead movement." The denominator of the tempo fraction was critical. Mistime your forward swing by a single frame and your drive peeled off into the trees.

I fast-forwarded to Tiger's tee shot on the par-5 thirteenth, a sweet little draw that traced the curve of the dogleg and found the middle of the fairway. Clicking the mouse to advance Tiger's swing frame by frame, I counted 19 frames to the top of his backswing and an additional 6 frames back to the ball.

"Nineteen?" Garrity's voice rose. "With a *fairway* metal?"

I shared his surprise. I had never seen Tiger get down to 19 frames with a long club. "Moe Norman was 18/6," I said, "but he had a much shorter swing."

"So which is it? Is Tiger a 21/7 or an 18/6?"

I gave Garrity my best scientific assessment: "I dunno."

———

I repeat, whether Tiger was a speedy 21/7 or a furiously fast 18/6 was immaterial. What mattered was his *tempo,* and both of his timed swings were pretty close to the 3-to-1 ideal. But I didn't know what to make of a world-class golfer who changed tempo the way other people changed radio stations. And it struck me, as I timed more swings, that Tiger still hit more good shots at 21/7 or 20/7 than he did with his denominator-6 swing. That one frame made a big difference on the downswing.

Woods finished T4 at the 2010 Masters. Which was incredible, given the length of his layoff, the tabloidization of his extra-marital affairs, and the fact that he seemed to have at least two mental clocks competing for his attention on every shot.

Later that spring, rumors spread that Tiger was going to fire Haney. Instead, his coach showed some deft timing of his own by dropping Woods as a client. Calling their relationship "dysfunctional," Haney told reporters that "six years is a long time. It wasn't going to last forever." He added, "If there wasn't a scandal, I think he'd be playing better golf."

Over the following months, Woods became his own range tutor, consulting from time to time with a brainiac swing coach named Sean Foley, who was already working with Justin Rose, Hunter Mahan, Sean O'Hair and Stephen Ames. Tiger's full-swing tempo showed some short-term improvement—enough that by mid-summer he displayed fewer of those 6-frame downswings and more swings that were within a frame or two of 21/7. (See his T4 finish in the U.S. Open at Pebble Beach.) His action looked smoother, and he started hitting the ball long and straight again.

On the greens, however, he was very much the post-scandal Tiger. Timing a number of his practice-green five-footers at the British Open in St. Andrews, I got 16/7, 17/9, and everything in-between. Tiger looked frustrated and grumpy. He changed putters between rounds, which was completely out of character.

But even I, tracking Tiger from week to week, couldn't have predicted his collapse, a couple of weeks later, at the WGC-Bridgestone Invitational. Playing on a Firestone South course that he had previously owned, in a tournament that he had won seven times, Woods shot 18-over par and wound up in a tie for 78th—the worst finish of his career. "It's Official," read one web headline. "Tiger Woods Has Lost His Game."

Tiger's tempo? Very poor. Long game, short game, everything was broken. I could no longer dodge the conclusion that Woods—the player I had singled out in *Tour Tempo* for having the best tempo in tournament golf—now had the *worst* tempo in tournament golf.

Tiger must have reached a few conclusions of his own. A few days later, he hired Sean Foley to be his swing coach.

———

"It's a process," Woods says of his struggles. "It doesn't happen overnight. I know it's in there, because I can hit some really sweet shots [but] it's a matter of more work, more reps, and more comfort. … Any time you make changes you want to go back to your old motor patterns, especially when you're under the gun."

Tiger may be missing the forest for the trees. Yes, it takes a lot of reps to consciously train your muscles to follow new patterns. That's why swing changes are so bad for tempo. Timing *has* to suffer when you're trying to control a position of your body while it is swinging an object at over 100 miles per hour. But if tempo is as critical to shotmaking as the pros say it is, you'd think that Tiger would practice his new moves *at his prescribed tempo*. Many pros, in fact, do just that.

Woods does not, as far as I can tell.

It would be self-serving for me to suggest that he perform his swing drills to a 21/7 Tour Tempo track. Plus, I could be totally wrong in my belief that *any* of Tiger's swings—whether molded by Harmon, Haney or Foley—will hit it long and straight when executed at a consistent 3-to-1 tempo.

And if I'm wrong, I'll admit it in *Tour Tempo 3: Timing is for Twits*.

But I don't think I'm wrong.

THE SHORT GAME

PART ONE

Chapter 1

A Rebel With Barely a Clue

"Golf's Last Secret Finally Revealed."

In 2001, I slapped that phrase on the cover of a spiral-bound instruction manual. The sixty-page manual, titled *Tour Pro Tempo,* introduced students at my VIP Golf Schools to a radical new approach to golf instruction. It was an approach that recognized tempo as a fundamental, not as a mere refinement of the golf swing. When it came time to collaborate on a book, my co-author, John Garrity, pointed out that the word "Pro" in the title was redundant; he suggested the more alliterative *Tour Tempo.* But John was adamant about keeping the subtitle. "No golfer," he said, "can read that claim on a book jacket without thumbing through the pages to satisfy his curiosity."

It was a great slogan, all right. A lot better than "Golf's Last Secret Mostly Revealed."

I'm not saying that *Tour Tempo* was anything less than the instructional breakthrough we advertised it to be. I'm just admitting that it shipped with a few parts missing. Specifically, *Tour Tempo* left readers with the impression that golf ended about 70 yards from the flagstick.

Some noticed the omission. "What about my short game?" asked a generic student in the FAQ chapter. "Does Tour Tempo apply to chip shots and short pitches?"

My written answer was terse:

> Yes, up to a point. Most tour players seem to swing at or near the 3-to-1 ratio when they are hitting from greenside bunkers or pitching to greens from 40 or more yards. It's a different story when they are chipping or hitting finesse shots from greenside rough. (Tiger Woods's chipping tempo is 15/7, or about 2-to-1.) My rule of thumb is: Anytime your backswing takes the club to a point where it is parallel or past parallel to the ground, Tour Tempo applies. If your shot doesn't require that long a backswing, you don't need a 3-to-1 swing.

Well, I got one thing right. Tiger Woods *does* chip to a 2-to-1 tempo. (Turns out most of the pros do.) But I must have been high on ryegrass when I told Garrity that tour players were 3-to-1 from bunkers. That was flat-out wrong. Phil Mickelson's wrist hinge on chip shots is so abrupt that his club is parallel to the ground before his hands have moved back a foot, and he is most definitely not swinging 3-to-1.

What can I say? When I began my tempo research, I wasn't too concerned about the short game. Like most golfers, I liked to hit the long ball. I loved the feel of a good drive, the crisp sound of impact, the beauty of the ball's climb, the way the ball hopped down the fairway upon landing. My SpeedBall training aid wasn't designed to help a trembling golfer make a three-foot putt; it was a proven tool for increasing clubhead speed. (Important on full shots. Not so important for strokes on or around the greens.) It didn't occur to me that tempo could be as big an issue with the shorter swings as it was with the longer swings. I timed a few of the tour pros' chip shots and putts. I determined that they did not conform to the 3-to-1 ratio. And then I stuffed the data in a file drawer.

Golf's last secret partly concealed.

———

It wasn't until we decided to develop the first of our digital audio players that I revisited the subject. "Why don't we take a look at the short game," I suggested to John Novosel Jr., "and see if something jumps out at us." So, starting with tournament telecasts in the spring of 2004, I began timing the shots that make up the short game—the putts, chips, pitches and bunker shots that the pros practice for hours on end.

When I say "timing," I don't mean with a stop watch. Digital video editors employ a frame counter—a little box in the editing window that tells you which individual image you are looking at when you "freeze the frame" or advance the video in stop-action mode. Since broadcast video is composed of 30 images per second, any one frame occupies the screen for a mere 33 thousandths of a second. That image has a specific "address" measured in minutes, seconds and frames. As the clubhead makes its first move away from the ball, for instance, the counter might read 0:11:21, meaning 11 seconds plus 21 frames of the following second.*

To time a swing, I clicked the mouse to advance the action frame by frame until I found the point where the clubhead appeared to be motionless.** I flagged that frame (or jotted its number down on a note pad) and then mouse-clicked the swing back to impact—the point where the clubface met the ball. From there it was simply a matter of subtraction to get the elapsed-frame counts for the backswing and forward swing. For example, when Tiger Woods chipped in for birdie on the par-3 16th hole during the final round of the 2005 Masters, his backswing consumed 16 frames of CBS video, while his forward swing used 8. I expressed that ratio as "16/8" (pronounced "sixteen-eight").

With the full swing, you may remember from *Tour Tempo,* I noticed that virtually every pro golfer from Bobby Jones to the present had a

---

*When I first started timing the pros, I had to transfer their swings to videotape and then digitize them for my computer—a time-consuming process. Now I simply hit the frame button on my DirecTV, and I'm ready to go. If it's high-definition video (60 frames per second), I divide each frame count by two. That way, I don't confuse readers who have gotten used to the Tour Tempo standards of "27/9", "24/8" and "21/7".

**The start of the swing is defined as the first frame where there is a discernible movement of the clubhead away from the ball. The end of the backswing is defined as the point where the clubhead appears motionless, neither continuing away from the ball nor starting back toward the ball. The start of the forward swing is defined as the first frame where the clubhead starts moving back toward the ball from the top. We allow a 1-frame differential (33 thousandths of a second) for difficult camera angles and operator judgment. Any frame count, in other words, is "plus or minus one frame."

takeaway-to-impact ratio of 3-to-1. Jones, who famously wrote that "nobody ever swung a golf club too slowly," got to impact in a brisk 1.2 seconds using the same 27/9 rhythm that Tiger Woods employed to win the 1997 Masters. Nancy Lopez, in her best years, was a 30/10. Seve Ballesteros and Sam Snead were 24/8, while Ben Hogan and Jack Nicklaus were 21/7. The typical mid- to high-handicapper, on the other hand, draws the club back slowly and self-consciously before lunging at the ball. That leads to inefficient ratios such as 34/9 or 25/10 and golf shots that fly off line or drop like wounded quail.

So we began to accumulate short-game data. And guess what? We discovered that there was a *two*-to-1 optimal tempo ratio for tour players on their shots from less than 60 yards.

I say "optimal" because the pros didn't seem to be as consistent with their putting, chipping and greenside bunker tempos as they were with their longer pitches and full swings. So while Woods clocks out at 16/8 when he's chipping and putting his best, I've timed him as slow as 18/9 (on a chip to save par at the 2010 Masters) and as fast as 14/8 (while four-putting the 15th green at the 2010 Quail Hollow Championship). Mickelson, similarly, times out at 15/8, 13/7, or 16/8, depending upon the shot he's attempting and whether or not he pulls it off.

Some of this deviation I attribute to the variability of the greenside environment. A downhill, down-grain putt may require no more than a 3-inch backswing, while a buried lie in the face of a bunker may call for a hands-above-the-shoulders swing and an audible grunt. Furthermore, the pros are trying to execute these mostly-delicate shots under tournament pressure. That explains how Stewart Cink—who putted to a dependable 14/7 tempo to defeat Tom Watson at the 2009 British Open—could 13/6-yip a five-foot birdie putt on the sixteenth at Celtic Manor near the end of the 2010 Ryder Cup. Pressure, as any heart-in-his-throat Ryder Cup veteran will tell you, is a tempo killer.

But as we timed more and more short swings, we noticed that the denominators in the tempo fraction tended to be our old friends—7, 8, and 9. That meant that, contrary to what one would expect, the forward swing on a 20-foot chip took as long to execute as the forward swing on a 300-yard drive.

("That's crazy," I told my son Scott, who was an early test subject. "I feel like Galileo when he dropped objects with different weights off the Leaning Tower of Pisa.") The nominators, however, were significantly lower, 14 to 20 being a typical frame count for a greenside backswing. That had logic on its side, because a backswing where the clubhead stopped at belt level wouldn't take as much time as a backswing where the clubhead reached a point high above the golfer's head.

Or would it? The downswing data told us one thing: Elapsed time is not proportionate to the distance the hands and clubhead travel. The backswing data suggested the opposite: Elapsed time IS proportionate to the distance the hands and clubhead travel.

If Einstein had been alive and answering FAQs, I'd have sent him an e-mail asking if his Theory of Relativity applied to flop shots. In his absence, I simply accepted that we were dealing with much slower clubhead speeds in the short game.

———

Why slower clubhead speeds? It sounds like a dumb question, but it would be dumber not to answer it. Assuming a square face at impact (and disregarding launch angle and spin rate), there is a direct correlation between clubhead speed at impact and the distance a golf ball flies. A tour pro gets over 200 yards of carry with his 5-iron because his clubhead is going 106 miles per hour when it meets the ball. A lesser athlete, with only 90 mph of clubhead speed at his disposal, must settle for 170 yards of carry. Clubhead speed is the principal power ingredient in golf.

But power is rarely a consideration from 100 yards in. At that range, you're looking for accuracy. And with the exception of specialty shots like the skyscraper-lob or the sand shot from a buried lie, a short, slow swing tends to be more accurate than a long, fast swing.

Theory aside, I found that tour players tend to putt, chip and pitch with an action that is two parts backswing to one part forward swing. The following table shows the four most common elapsed times and frames ratios and some pros who employ those tempos on most of their short shots:

20/10 (1.0 second)	18/9 (.90 seconds)	16/8 (.80 seconds)	14/7 (.70 seconds)
Padraig Harrington David Toms Charley Hoffman	Y.E. Yang Luke Donald Bill Haas	Tiger Woods Steve Marino Graeme McDowell	Jonathan Byrd Rickie Fowler Edoardo Molinari

As mentioned above, the appearance of 7s, 8s and 9s at the bottom of so many tempo fractions suggested that the denominator was the magic number. "Maybe every better-than-scratch golfer has one elapsed time for the forward stroke," Garrity suggested, "no matter what club he's using, no matter how near or how distant his target. If Pro X is a 21/7 off the tee, he'll be a 14/7 from the fringe. And maybe he's 17/7 from 50 yards out, the frame count for his backswing varying according to the length of his backswing."

It was an elegant theory, but the data shot it full of holes. Some pros do, indeed, time out the same on their longer downswings as they do on their shorter downswings. Tiger Woods was a consistent 3-to-1, 24/8 with his woods and irons when he won the 2000 U.S. Open by fifteen strokes, and he was an equally-consistent 2-to-1, 16/8 with his putter. The denominator on almost all of his forward swings, regardless of their length, was 8 frames, or about 0.266 seconds. Applying Garrity's "Universal Theory of Golf Tempo," we could have called Tiger an "8" and predicted that his 50- to 100-yard wedge shots would launch to an in-between tempo of 18/8, 20/8, or 22/8. But it turns out—and here's where I had to send my astute co-author back to his laptop—that there are very few "in-between" tour tempos, very few 2.5-to-1 fractions that correspond to half- or three-quarter-length swings. Tiger's golf shots conformed to either his full-swing tempo (24/8) or his short-game tempo (16/8). He didn't mess with Mr. In-Between.

Anyway, most tour players don't employ the same forward-swing timing for all their strokes. When 19-year-old Rory McIlroy shot a final-round 62 to win the 2010 Quail Hollow Championship, he was a patient 16/8 with his putter and a lightning-fast 19/6 with his power clubs. (Or if you prefer, McIlroy was a methodical Dr. Jekyll when he had to hole a slippery 8-footer for birdie, but he turned into a hyperactive Mr. Hyde when his caddie handed him the driver.) Meanwhile, Phil Mickelson employs different short-game tempos depending on the shot. When he won the 2010 Masters, Mickelson hit putts, chips and pitches that timed out at 15/7, 16/8, 13/6, 14/7, 18/9, and practically every other possible 2-to-1 variation. His full swings, however, were a consistent 21/7, give or take a frame.

Conclusion: *World-class players, when they are playing their best, adhere to a 2-to-1 tempo constant on shots from 60 yards in. However, the time it takes a given player to execute those shots is not necessarily linked to the player's full-swing tempo. The shorter swings can be significantly faster or slower than the longer swings, depending on the individual.*

I can't say I was shocked. My previous tempo research had taught me to distrust conventional wisdom about the golf swing—cliches such as "low and slow" and "tempo matches temperament." The full-swing data proved that tour players took the club back much faster than amateurs did. The full-swing data also showed no correlation between a player's tempo and his height, weight, speed-of-play, speech patterns, Type-A tendencies, credit history or political leanings. To the consternation of most teaching pros—not to mention the tour pros themselves—the full-swing data revealed that, at the top levels of the game, *tempo isn't even an individual trait.* Virtually all tour players, be they fast-swingers or slow-swingers, swing to the same 3-to-1 tempo.

So no, I wasn't shocked by any of the short-game results. I wasn't, that is, until I started timing shots from greenside bunkers. And then, oh boy.

———

Consider the fearsome sand shot.

I say "fearsome" because most mid-to-high handicappers will tell you they have absolutely no faith in their ability to pull off a simple explosion shot. Short-game coach Dave Pelz, who polled thousands of golfers for his book, *Golf Without Fear,* put the greenside bunker shot at No. 2 on his "Most Feared Shots" list, second only to the dreaded short putt. "And our survey golfers," Pelz wrote, "weren't talking about extra-difficult plugged lies in the sand, awkward stances or shots with super-long carries over dangerous trouble areas. Their fear was of hitting an ordinary greenside bunker shot from a good lie, the kind the tour pros are often thinking about holing."

Here's the conventional wisdom about this scary shot: *You have to hit it hard.* Or rather, you have to hit the *sand* hard. Every golfer who's read even one golf magazine knows that you don't try to hit the *ball* in a greenside bunker, you try to displace the sand under the ball and propel the whole ensemble out of the bunker and onto the green. That requires considerable force and, it stands to reason, considerable clubhead speed. It follows, then, that the tour pros must hit their bunker shots with the 3-to-1 tempo that they employ for their other three-quarter and full-swing shots.

Guess what? *They don't.*

I timed Birdie Kim holing a long greenside bunker shot on the final hole at the Broadmoor Resort to win the 2005 U.S. Women's Open. Her tempo fraction was 18/9. I timed Paul Azinger jarring his bunker shot on the 72nd hole to beat Payne Stewart at the 1993 Memorial. Paul's tempo fraction was 19/8 (with a backswing so short he could have practiced it in a portalet). I timed Bob Tway holing out an equally abbreviated final-hole explosion shot to steal the 1986 PGA Championship from Greg Norman. Tway's winning rhythm? A patient 21/10.

Not 3-to-1. More like *two*-to-1. The pros hit their bunker shots to the same tempo they used for chip shots and putts.

I was amazed. How could a ten-foot putt and a forty-foot sand shot have the same tempo? It's totally counter intuitive. You're talking about a stroke of a few inches length, which, if applied to your ankle, wouldn't raise a bruise, versus a stroke in which the clubhead travels ten feet or more and approaches speeds of up to 50 miles per hour. And consider this: When we caught a tour pro hitting a standard bunker shot with a tempo that was closer to his 3-to-1 full-shot rhythm—20/7, say, or 26/8—the ball was usually chunked onto the fringe or bladed over the green. Rickie Fowler, at a tournament at Torrey Pines, took an 18/6 swing in a bunker and flew the green by 20 yards. (The startled announcer said, "It's safe to say that will qualify as the surprise of the day.") At another tournament, Natalie Gulbis took a 31/8 whack at the ball and rolled her sand shot to the other end of the green. (Announcer: "She didn't get any spin on that ball.")

The professionals, even with their perfected and practiced short-game techniques, suffered the same bad outcomes as their Wednesday pro-am partners when they got the tempo wrong.

———

To complete the picture, we needed to know what rhythm amateurs were using when forced to hit out of sand. To find out, we shot video of low-, mid-, and high-handicap golfers practicing their sand shots at Kansas City-area golf clubs. Back in the studio, we applied our standard frame-counting technique to the videos and sorted the results by tempo ratios—so many into 14/7, so many into 18/7, so many into 21/7, etc. It didn't take long to conclude that the amateur tempos were nothing like the pro tempos. The amateur bunker backswings varied greatly, taking as few as 14 frames and as many as 30 frames to reach the top, followed by an equally arbitrary forward swing of from 6 to 10 frames. To the extent that the data fit any profile, it showed the amateurs swinging in the 3-to-1 and 4-to-1 tempo ranges. Only a few of these swings deposited the ball in close proximity to the hole.

No matter. By the end of 2004 I had collected enough data to conclude that Tour Tempo in the short-game consisted of two aspects.

Aspect number one is the *ratio* of (A) the elapsed time it takes a player to start and finish the backswing compared with (B) the elapsed time it takes to get back to impact from the start of the forward swing. This universal short-game ratio is 2-to-1. It takes twice as long for a player to get from the start of the backswing to the end of the backswing compared to the time it takes to get from the start of the forward swing to impact. This can be expressed in frames of video as 14/7, 16/8, 18/9, and 20/10.

Aspect number two is the *amount* of elapsed time, measured in hundredths of a second, that it takes the club to go from the start of the backswing to impact. Four different elapsed times correspond to the four different ratios. Seventy hundredths (0.70) corresponds to 14/7. Eighty hundredths (0.80) corresponds to 16/8. Ninety hundredths (0.90) corresponds to 18/9. One second (1.00) corresponds to 20/10.

Armed with that information, I returned to my video editor and produced short-game audio tracks for an old-fashioned audio cassette player. These ten tracks consisted of the Tour Tempo training tones for the four new tempos in two formats—the familiar *beep ... beep-beep* or the spoken *"Swing! ... Set! Through!"* As I had learned to do for the full-swing tones, I allowed one-fifth of a second for reaction time to the first tone and then moved the second tone forward by a fifth of a second to signal the change of direction into the forward swing. The third tone (impact) stayed put, since it was a timing target, not a stimulus requiring a response.

Once the short-game tones were loaded onto my cassette player, I strapped my clubs to a golf cart and drove up the winding path to the hilltop end of the Hallbrook Country Club practice range.

It was time for a test drive. Or rather, a test chip.

Chapter 2

The Tempo Trials

The Tom Fazio-designed range at Hallbrook Country Club is the best practice facility in Kansas City. Situated on a hill that climbs to the setting sun, the tree-lined range has generous zoysia tees at each end and attractive target greens set into the slope. Just north of the upper tee line is a two-tiered practice green with 5,000-square feet of pampered bentgrass for putting, a luxurious mane of zoysia for chipping and pitching, and a greenside bunker as spacious and well maintained as any on the course.

It was up to this practice green that I drove my cart on a beautiful morning in 2004. Along with my clubs I had a cassette player loaded with my new short-game tones. Nobody was on the green, so I put down the cassette player, advanced the tape to the 18/9 tones, and began rolling ten-footers toward the nearest hole. My prototype putter, with its yellow, plastic head, resembled a half-moon of Colby cheese, but it had a sweet spot the size of a lemon.

This wasn't rocket science. It wasn't even putting science. I simply wanted to try out the short-game tones before testing them on volunteers.

I putted to the *"Swing! ... Set! Through!"* of the 18/9 track for about ten minutes, holing a good percentage. I then moved to the fringe and began chipping to the tones with a pitching wedge. The Tour Tempo chipping stroke seemed slow, but I had no difficulty executing the shot. My years of swinging to the full-swing tones made it second-nature.

But when I strolled into the greenside bunker with my lob wedge, my short-game sensibilities took a sudden and unexpected hit. My first swing to the 18/9 tones seemed to take forever, but the clubhead hit the sand before I heard the impact note. My first thought was, "Man, that's slow. That *can't* be right."

My next couple of swings must have been pretty close to 18/9 because my clubhead hit the sand on the word "through," and the ball popped out of the bunker and onto the green with a minimal scattering of sand. But I'd have sworn the sand came out of an hourglass. To nail the impact tone I had to practically let the clubhead fall back to the sand.

"Are you kidding me?" I stared at the cassette player, which kept issuing the swing-set-through command in my middle son's calm but authoritative voice. A third voice, the one in my head, said *Nobody can swing a club that slowly.*

Was I grinning? Probably.

With Tour Tempo, you'll remember, the eureka moment came when you swung to the full-swing tones for the first time and felt as if you were a 33-rpm vinyl record playing at 45-rpm. "I can't swing that fast!" was the standard lament of our test subjects, most of whom had perfected the "low and slow" takeaway favored by over-analytical teaching pros. But now, in the Hallbrook practice bunker, I cried "Eureka!" over the flip side of the tempo equation: *Amateur swings are too fast for ordinary bunker play.*

Yeah, I was definitely grinning.

———

I'll have more to say about the bunker game—including a few set-up suggestions that will greatly simplify your technique—in the chapter titled "Sand Play." If you're impatient, and if you think your technique is reasonably sound, skip what follows and go directly to **TourTempo.com/multimedia** to download the Tour Tempo short-game tones and video tutorials. Watch John Novosel Jr.'s sand-game tutorial, then go out to the nearest practice bunker and try out the different short-game tempos. See how long it takes you to get comfortable with the knife-through-butter stroke the pros use from greenside sand.

The beauty of Tour Tempo is that you don't have to understand the theory behind it to make it work for you. To borrow a line from Nike: *Just do it.*

For many of us, though, the whys and hows of good golf are almost as interesting as the game itself. That's why Ben Hogan's *Five Lessons* continues to sell. It's why a book called *Tiger's New Swing* was published in 2005. It's why a couple of Yale professors fact-checked *Tour Tempo* with a slightly more technical monograph titled, "Towards a Biomechanical Understanding of Tempo in the Golf Swing."

To wring more insight out of our short-game data, we turned to a readily-available pool of questioning golfers: the students at our Tour Tempo VIP Schools. These schools, conducted on an irregular basis, draw golfers from around the world. For their money, the tempo pilgrims now get two days of personal instruction from John Jr. and me; before-and-after FlightScope swing analysis; a fitness evaluation; the SpeedBall and Power Tools swing trainers; and a Tour Tempo Micro Player to complete their tempo overhaul.

Most of the VIP Schools are held at the Alvamar Golf Course in Lawrence, Ks. Alvamar is the training facility for the University of Kansas golf team and is one of the top practice facilities in the midwest. In addition to its two golf courses, its three practice tees and its "Night and Day" indoor practice building, Alvamar has a 7,000 square-foot tiered practice green that accommodates approach shots of up to 140 yards. We couldn't have built a better laboratory for our short-game experiments.

We started small: 3-foot putts. Having already shot video of the students putting to their usual tempos, we now had them stroke the same putts to the short-game tones. It quickly became evident that the putter, with its short and relatively slow stroke, was the perfect club for introducing students to Tour Tempo. The players learned not to anticipate the first and second tones, but to react to them—something that beginners can have trouble with on full swings. Opening with the putter also ratcheted down the "ball strike anxiety" that students invariably experience when asked to smack real golf balls. A 3-foot putt may be scary when you need to hole it for a par, but it won't turn your knuckles white when you're just rehearsing the stroke.

Just to be clear, a few of our test subjects were pretty close to the ideal putting tempo before we put them on the tones—more, certainly, than we saw with our full-swing students. A 24-handicap businessman from Milwaukee was 15/7. A retired engineer with a 5 handicap was a perfect 16/8. More typical, however, were the mid-to-high handicappers with putting strokes ranging from 14/5 to 20/6. Most of our VIPs were too fast into the ball, a jabby rhythm better suited to carpentry. And unlike the best putters on tour, who begin their forward strokes with minimal delay, our amateurs tended to end their takeaways with a pronounced pause. A few froze their backstrokes for a full two or three frames, as if posing for photographers.

A minute or two with the short-game tones was all it took to straighten them out. In hindsight, I wish we had scored our test subjects on the percentage of putts made, because they were observably more accurate when they putted to the tones. Lip-outs and complete misses were common in the "before" videos, but Tour Tempo putts rolled end over end into the cup.

"When you get the tempo right," I remember one of our VIP students saying, "the putter face seems to square itself." Whereas trying to square the putter face usually resulted in a "handsy" putt with off-center contact, sidespin and poor distance control.

"Exactly," I replied.

————

When we asked our VIP students to chip to the tones, we began to get some resistance. "I can't swing that slow," one fellow said, frowning over the scuff marks he'd left on the fringe with his first three efforts. His "before" chips had a get-it-over-with urgency, the spasmodic forward stroke ending with a decisive hammering of the club onto the ball and into the turf. The short-game tones, however, left him with all this forward-stroke time to kill—time that he filled by literally stopping his club on the downswing and then re-starting, a move that had him hitting the ground a good three inches behind the ball. It wasn't until I pointed out that he could take a longer backswing that he began to get a sense of the proper rhythm.

"It almost feels like gravity is bringing the club down," I called out to all the students within earshot. "Like you're doing nothing."

On his next swing, he nailed the tempo tones. The range ball vaulted off his clubface with a solid click, hopped onto the green, rolled some thirty feet with a right-to-left curve, and ended up a few feet from the hole.

"That's pretty damn good," he said.

His very next attempt he chunked, but five or ten more minutes with the tones had him chipping with a consistency he had never displayed in his golfing life. But the slowness of the stroke still had him shaking his head. Like most weekend golfers, he found the pros' chipping tempo to be entirely foreign. He hated to see the clubhead stray too far from the safety of his setup position, and once he'd started his backswing he wanted to return the club to the ball as quickly as possible.

"I've tried just about every chipping technique known to man," he told me afterwards. "Ball in the center, ball back, ball off the toe. Standard grip, putting grip. Everything I've tried worked for that one day, when I had a pro talking me through it. Some even told me that my tempo was screwed up, but they didn't have a fix for tempo. And now this."

I shrugged and smiled. I didn't know if Tour Tempo really worked with the short game. Besides, if he thought the short-game tempos felt slow on a chip, he'd freak when he got to the sand.

I said, "Let's go to the bunker."

———

Funny thing about the sand game. Some of our test subjects did, indeed, find Tour Tempo to be "rather slow," "quite slow" or "ridiculously slow." But equally as many didn't voice an opinion one way or the other. The incontrovertible fact was this: none of the self-described bad bunker players had a "before" sand-game tempo of around 2-to-1, like the tour pros. The amateurs tried to dig their balls out of bunkers with 3-to-1 frame counts such as 19/6, 21/8 or 27/9—tempos, ironically, that work for full-swing shots, but "crash and burn" from the sand. Their fast bunker swings produced the full array of shots we've all hit from greenside bunkers—bladed into the bunker face; skulled over the green; shanked into the adjoining bunker; chunked onto the grassy bank, the ball rolling back into the sand.

Comparing videos of professional and amateur bunker shots, it struck me that the pros have been telling us something very specific when they call the sand shot "the easiest shot in golf." The pro swing is literally easy—as in relaxed, unhurried. It's not a strike or a blow. It's more of a caress.

Conversely, our VIP test subjects swung *hard*—harder, in many cases, than they would swing for a fairway shot from ten times the distance. Clearly they were operating under the assumption that extra energy is required to dig under a ball and propel both ball and a hefty slice of sand onto a green.

Because sand is heavy. (See "sandbags.")

Imagine our surprise, then, when we began to measure clubhead speeds on straightforward sand shots, comparing the amateurs to the pros. The typical 15-handicapper slings his wedge into the sand at full speed, moving the ball about four feet. Luke Donald, meanwhile, hits the same shot with around 50 to 60 percent of his normal swing speed ... and leaves his ball four inches from the hole.

This was a huge discovery. For one thing, it meant that bad bunker players weren't bad because they lacked the strength or flexibility to hit from sand. Any golfer can achieve a clubhead speed of 45 mph. Furthermore, it meant that the explosion shot fit the Tour Tempo paradigm of tempo determining technique, rather than the other way around. How you hit a bunker shot is obviously important, but no more important than the pace of the swing.

Tempo is a fundamental for every shot in the bag.

———

I could go on and on, telling you how our VIP Golf School subjects performed on fairway pitches, bump-and-run shots, bellied wedges and greenside lobs— but that would be redundant. All our short-game trials showed the amateurs swinging the clubhead considerably faster than the pros, especially on the forward swing. But with the aid of the short-game tones, our amateurs quickly obtained "tour tempo" and saw immediate, dramatic improvement.

As with the full-swing version of Tour Tempo, the critical element seems to be the tones' ability to instill the feel of a properly-executed short-game stroke. Which takes us back to my hero, Percy Boomer. "One sensation for all shots" is how Boomer described the feel-based method in his 1942 instructional, *On Learning Golf.* He added: "The only way in which we can repeat correct shots time after time is to be able to repeat the correct feel of how they are produced."

The Tempo Trials proved to my satisfaction that Tour Tempo works for the short game as well as it works for the full swing, and for the same reason: *It's all about feel.*

To begin applying Tour Tempo to your shots around the green, proceed to the next chapter.

Chapter 3

Putting

Tempo isn't everything on the greens. It's the only thing.

Vince Lombardi didn't say that. I did.

To emphasize the point, I'm going to withhold my putting lecture for a couple of pages and ask you to grab a putter and a few golf balls and find a spot where you can practice. (An actual green would be ideal, but the living room rug will do.) You'll also need to pay a quick visit to **TourTempo.com/multimedia** to download the short-game tones and instructional videos.

We're going to start with your putting stroke, since it's the easiest way to learn how to use the tones. Don't worry about hitting to a target. Just make sure that all your movements are smooth, and not jerky.

When you first start your selected ratio, a series of three repetitive tones will play.

- On the first tone, start swinging your putter back.
- The second tone is your cue to start swinging forward to impact.
- The third tone corresponds to impact. Try to time your forward swing so that "impact" and the third tone are simultaneous.

So, to begin, select a short-game tempo. Your choices are:

- 20/10. The slowest of the four Tour Tempo short-game ratios, this is the putting rhythm employed by Padraig Harrington and David Toms.
- 18/9. This is the putting rhythm employed by Luke Donald and Y. E. Yang. It's also the rhythm we recommend you start with.
- 16/8. The most common putting tempo among male tour pros, this is the putting rhythm employed by Tiger Woods and Graeme McDowell.
- 14/7. The fastest of the Tour Tempo short-game ratios, this is the putting rhythm employed by Rickie Fowler and Edoardo Molinari.

Experiment with the four different ratios in order to find the one that gives you the best feeling of square contact. Eventually you'll want to putt to a target and fine tune your selection. It always goes back to this rule—use the ratio that gives you the best results on a three to five foot putt.

I'll say it again: Good putting tempo is invariable. If your optimal stroke is 18/9, you should time out at .90 seconds from takeaway to impact on every one of your putts. It doesn't matter if the putt is a four-footer or a cross-country lag putt. The tempo stays the same.

How long a stroke should you be taking? I'd say six inches of backswing is about right. Or four inches. Or sixteen. The length of your backswing can vary, but the tempo stays the same.

This is the putting secret that the pros haven't really tried to keep. That's because, until a decade ago, even the best putters didn't understand how critical tempo was to their success. In his 1979 book, *The Short Way to Lower Scoring,* two-time PGA champ Paul Runyan devoted 43 pages of cogent technical analysis to the art of putting—including roughly 3,500 words on "Choosing a Putter"—without once mentioning tempo or timing. Twenty-two years later, in an instructional titled *No More Bad Shots,* Hank Haney covered the subject in two short sentences. ("Good putters have a smooth tempo. Poor putters tend to rush the transition from back to through stroke.") The idea that rhythm might be a putting fundamental was not a part of mainstream teaching.

To change the putting paradigm, somebody—not a busy touring pro—had to do some actual research. That somebody turned out to be a one-time tour aspirant and former NASA scientist named Dave Pelz, founder of the Pelz Golf

Institute, a short-game academy. Pelz isolated the invariable tempo principle while working with a putting robot of his own design. The robot, nicknamed "Perfy," rolled balls to the hole with a "pure-in-line stroke"—Pelz's term for a stroke based on pendulum motion. "The rhythm of a pendulum," Pelz wrote, "is the same regardless of its swing length. That's why we use grandfather clocks to tell time, because as the lengths of their swings decay, the timing of their swing motions remain constant."

Perfy turned out to be one hell of a putter. Once aimed correctly, Pelz's robot was nearly 100% accurate, thanks to a linkage that kept the putter face square to the aim line throughout the stroke. But accuracy also requires the consistent application of power, which Perfy achieved by swinging like a pendulum from a fixed suspension point. The lengths of the swings were variable, depending on distance to the hole and green conditions, but every swing—measured from the top of the backswing to the end of the follow-through—timed out at exactly 0.70 seconds.

"How does this relate to your putting?" Pelz asked. "Simple. Your stroke should always take the same amount of time and should always move at the same rhythm, for all putts, regardless of putt length or the length of your stroke." And if you weren't willing to take his word for that—on the reasonable objection that his robot had never cashed a check on the PGA Tour—Pelz had proprietary data proving that the game's best players swung to an internal clock that did not vary from putt to putt. Ben Crenshaw's rhythm was consistent. Tiger Woods's rhythm used to be consistent. Brad Faxon's rhythm was consistent.

"Rhythm is the glue of these great strokes," Pelz concluded. "Good setup, alignment, touch, feel, green-reading and stroke mechanics are all necessary for good putting. But without a constant and repeatable rhythm … you will never become a great putter. Never. And that's a fact."

———

Left unanswered was the next question: What is the ideal putting rhythm?

After all, having a "constant and repeatable rhythm" won't make you a good putter if that rhythm is two parts backswing to four parts forward swing. (Deceleration is one of the worst putting faults.) Furthermore, the pendulum analogy only takes you so far. Real golfers don't hold the putter head off the ground and then release the whole arms-shoulder-club assembly, letting gravity pull the clubface down to the ball. Real golfers have backswings.

Fortunately, Tour Tempo answers the rhythm question unequivocally: The ideal putting rhythm is 2-to-1.

This is not a matter of individual preference. It's not some teaching pro's prescription. This is simply what the best putters do. Tiger Woods, when he's putting well, is a consistent 16/8. Lee Westwood, when he goes around in 26 putts, is a steady 14/7. Conversely, when a touring pro misses a short putt or leaves himself ten feet from the hole on a lengthy putt, it is usually because his rhythm is irregular. The 8-foot putt that 59-year-old Tom Watson missed on the 72nd hole of the 2009 British Open? That was a 12/8 stab. (Compare that to his 16/8 tempo when he was sinking them from everywhere on the green.) David Toms' agonizing miss from 42 inches on the first playoff hole at the 2011 Players Championship? That was a yippy 15/12. (Compare that to his 19/9 tempo on the 20-foot putt he made on the 72nd hole to get into the playoff.)

The 2-to-1 putting rhythm is a revelation to most of my VIP students. "The stroke feels smooth," is a typical reaction from a student putting to the short-game tones for the first time. Or, "I can feel the tension leaving my hands and forearms." Some students notice that the ball behaves differently on its way to the cup. "I'm getting that end-over-end roll instead of the hooky-slicey path I'm used to. My distance control is better, too."

———

Then you've got Bob Grober, a professor of applied physics at Yale University.

"There are three fundamental observations regarding the putting stroke of proficient golfers," Grober states in the introduction to his 2009 study, "Resonance in Putting."

> The first is the observation that the putter head is moving at constant speed as it impacts the ball.

> The second observation is that the total duration (i.e. length of time) of the putting stroke is relatively insensitive to the length of the putt (i.e. the intended initial velocity of the ball).

The final observation is that the ratio of the duration of the backswing, *tb,* to the duration of the downswing, *td,* in the putting stroke is close to two, *tb/td* ≈ 2.

Grober's first point, about the speed of the putter head being constant through impact, explodes another golf myth—the old bromide about good putters accelerating the clubhead through impact. His other two observations confirm the findings of Pelz (the same stroke duration for putts of all lengths) and myself (the 2-to-1 ratio).

The most interesting aspect of Grober's very scientific study is his conclusion that the Holy Grail of putting is "the putter head … moving at constant speed as it impacts the ball." This constant speed at impact, he argues, is what separates the pro from the amateur. It's the alchemy that delivers the putter face square to the ball at impact. It's the magic that enables great putters like Ben Crenshaw and Brad Faxon to control the speed of their putts. It's the secret sauce of feel.

And how do the pros manage to strike their putts with a clubhead that is neither accelerating nor decelerating? Simple. They stroke all their putts, regardless of length, in an identical time frame (Pelz) with a consistent 2-to-1 rhythm (Novosel).

Tempo ≈ Feel

———

Ready for some good news? You don't have to understand the science behind the resonant putting stroke to put it to use. Luke Donald, a pretty smart guy, is the world's top-ranked golfer as this is written, but Grober's math is way beyond him. Bubba Watson may know his way around a square root, but only if it's embedded in sandy soil. Yet both of those guys can roll a golf ball across 60 feet of closely-mowed bentgrass and have it snuggle up close to the hole. Their secret? Tempo.

Practicing to the Tour Tempo tones will set your inner clock to the scientifically-validated 2-to-1 rhythm. The tones will also take your attention away from the mechanics of the stroke, which most great putters agree is critical.

Frequently Asked Questions

What's the best putting thought?

That's purely individual, but I'll tell you mine. And, actually, it's a 'feel'—not a thought. The 'feel' I get is that the ball is attached to the putter face (as it actually is when I practice with my Electric Putter), and I gauge how much effort it will take to toss it to the hole. That gives me the feeling of how long a stroke I should take. From the beginning of the stroke to impact, I just 'feel' the connection of the ball on the clubface, and as I do that, my right brain automatically figures out how much effort I'll need to get the ball to the hole.

In other words, I try to duplicate the *feel* of using the Electric Putter: a small forward press to pick up the ball ... the sensation of the ball being attached to the putter head ... and the same action that I have been practicing. What I *don't* want on a pressure putt is a lot of distracting thoughts about the mechanics of the stroke itself. I just duplicate the steady, flowing motion that I have been practicing with the tones.

I've never putted better in my life.

My biggest putting problem is distance control. Any ideas?

I learned something that helps with that back in 1988 at one of the golf academies I attended. Position yourself on the putting green about six feet away from the fringe. Take three balls and toss them underhanded so that they end up somewhere in the fringe. Then move back to 16 or 18 feet and toss the three balls with the same goal of having them end up in the fringe. Finally, repeat the drill using your putter instead of your hand. This will get your distances down and give you a feel for how fast the greens are that day.

I still like this for a warmup. Once you've got that feel for distance, take some normal putts and get the ball into the hole.

Remember, putting is totally a right-brain function. If you get too analytical when practicing, it will carry over to your stroke when you play.

But if I can't get analytical when I practice, how am I going to improve?

Glad you asked. *Simulation* is the answer. Astronauts do it. Even robots do it. It has something to do with the "hierarchical neural network for the control of and learning of voluntary movement," but I'll explain it in everyday English.

And here I'm talking about a specific kind of simulation: the *Karate Kid* way of learning. ("Wax on/Wax off.") That's what Mr. Miyagi had Daniel doing— performing needed motions of the body without consciously trying to learn the mechanics of those motions. Daniel waxed the car, painted the fence and sanded floors; motions identical to the karate moves, but in a different framework.

You might not get the distinction, but it's an important one. If you obsess about putting and you perform left-brain drills on the putting green for hours on end, that's how you'll putt when you play. It's Psychology 101. *Green grass ... white ball ... sunshine ... over-analytical thinking.* When you face a real putt with those same conditions, your mind will launch into the micromanagement of the stroke.

Our Electric Putter is a "Wax on/Wax off" putting simulator. You learn the feel of the motion, and then, by recreating the feel, you recreate the motion. You just do it.

Chapter 4

Chipping and Pitching

The chip shot can be the most exasperating shot in golf. You make a tiny backswing, your body stays relatively still, and the hole is so close you could easily toss the ball to it. But most mid-to-high handicappers are so afraid of chipping that they putt from well off the green to avoid the embarrassment of a shank, chunk or skull with a lofted club.

Hall of Fame third-baseman George Brett used to be one of those guys, despite his 3 handicap. "I had the chipping yips really bad a few years back," he told Golf.com in 2010. "If I knew I was going to play, within three minutes of waking up I'd start thinking, *Oh god, I have to chip today.*" Brett's demon yips left him when he took a few weeks off from golf, but he still worried about his short game. "Sometimes I'd be 20 feet off the green, and I'd putt it. Sure, it might take me three to get down. But if I chipped, it might take me four."

Brett, it goes without saying, knew *how* to chip. He's an avid golfer, and your avid golfer has read every how-to article and taken lessons on chipping fundamentals. Brett understood that his hands had to lead through the shot, that his weight should be forward with the ball slightly back in his stance, and that he shouldn't have a death grip on the club. He knew all that, but he continued to leave his chips way short or run them well past the hole. He said, "It was all in my head."

More likely, it was in his timing. When Brett executed his chip shot at the Tour Tempo ratio—two parts backswing to one part forward swing—the ball came off the clubface with a satisfying *click*, achieved its optimum trajectory, and rolled straight toward the target upon landing. But when Brett got the tempo wrong—when he yielded to anxiety and stabbed at the ball with, say, a 12/8 swing—he caught the leading edge of his club in the grass or he bounced the sole into the ball, producing an ankle-blazer that shot across the green.

George Brett, you're probably thinking, is not a golf pro. His chipping technique may be faulty, or maybe he doesn't handle pressure well. (Although Goose Gossage and a .331 lifetime batting average suggest the opposite.) Whatever the explanation, you find it implausible that poor tempo alone can cause a clubhead traveling as little as two feet to misfire so badly.

———

So let's look at the chipping of a PGA Tour pro. Better yet, let's look at the chipping of the tour pro whose short game has been described as "the best of all time," the lob-wedge virtuoso who hit a flop shot over a flinching Dave Pelz from five feet away, the star of the best-selling instructional video, *Secrets of the Short Game*—Phil Mickelson.

Lefty, I think we can agree, is a genius from fifty yards in. His three Masters titles testify to that. His technique is unorthodox—he plays the ball slightly forward in his stance and favors the lob wedge for most greenside shots—but he has total command of spin and trajectory. He can make his ball pop above his head and drop back down at his feet. He can make a knee-high pitch shot stop on a dime or release and run a hundred feet. Given the right lie and stance, he can even hit a pitch shot backwards over his head. What's more, Mickelson can perform these feats under pressure. Needing to birdie the 72nd hole to win the 2005 PGA Championship at Baltusrol, he cooly pitched from greenside rough to within two feet of the hole to win his second major. (His tempo on the pitch? A perfect 16/8.)

But even Mickelson sometimes flubs a chip. At the 2008 PGA Championship at Oakland Hills, Mickelson surprised his gallery by blading a chip shot across the 17th green. On the weekend, when he seemed to be making a move, he flat-out chili-dipped a couple of his patented flop shots and dropped out of contention. I remember how shocked the commentators were. They couldn't understand how a guy with Mickelson's skills could miss a green from twenty feet away.

Mickelson couldn't believe it, either. And if he studied the video of those bad shots afterwards, he might not have spotted any obvious flaws in his technique. It was his *rhythm* that was off. That skulled chip shot, for example, timed out at 16/6. That's two frames faster into impact than Mickelson's standard chipping tempo. The man with the greatest short game in history was blading and chunking greenside shots because he was rushing his forward swing.

To make certain I wasn't conflating cause and effect, I timed some of Mickelson's good chips at Oakland Hills. In the first round, for instance, he had chipped in from the frog hair to birdie the eighteenth hole. His frame count for that shot was 15/8. *Tour Tempo.*

Conclusion: Phil Mickelson's short-game slump was caused by a temporary inability to swing at the correct tempo.

––––––––

Granted, the weekend golfer's chipping yips may be due to genuine failures of technique. This lack of technique is actually caused by not knowing how this shot should feel. And instead of helping golfers get the correct feeling of the chip shot, they are given nostrums like: *"Stand closer to the ball with the heel of the club off the ground …. Employ a putting grip …. Play the ball off the toe of your right foot and lean toward the target to ensure a downward strike …. Stand taller …. Stand shorter …."* You get the idea. Some of these nostrums actually work. For a day or two.

Fortunately, you acquired the solution to your tempo problems when you purchased *Tour Tempo 2*. But before we program your internal short-game clock, we suggest that you perfect your chipping technique with a simple exercise called the "mini-Y drill." The mini-Y drill is ideal for practicing to the Tour Tempo short-game tones, and it forms the basis for the greenside shots demonstrated by John Novosel Jr. in the chipping video.* The mini-Y drill is

––––––––

*I say "forms the basis" because you must adjust your setup and swing for specific short-game challenges. When chipping, for example, you will usually have your feet closer together, you'll play the ball more in the middle of your stance, and your backswing will not be as "wide."

our preferred way of incorporating everything you need to learn about tempo and mechanics into your short game.

The Mini-Y Drill

1. Address   2. Top of Backswing   3. Impact   4. Finish

The "Y" in the mini-Y drill is formed by your club, arms and shoulders when you address the ball. Your goal in the mini-Y drill is to retain the Y while swinging the club back to the level of your waist and then forward again to a low finish. Maintaining the Y in this fashion gives structure to your setup and encourages a one-piece takeaway.

Your club, arms and shoulders form a Y at (1), the address position.

Maintain the structure of that Y as you move the club back to position (2), the top of the backswing. The Y will not be perfect when you get to this position, but do the best you can.

From (2) swing the club through (3), the impact position, to (4), the finish. Notice that the Y formed by the arms and shaft has been retained.

This drill looks simple and is simple, but it won't work its magic unless you get the position of the club right in three dimensions.

To start with, just walk through the mini-Y drill in slow motion, acquainting yourself with the correct positions of the club. Stop at (2) and take a look at the club. Then swing slowly through impact to the finish. *It is important that the club ends up exactly as shown.*

Once you have mastered these positions, go ahead and complete the mini-Y drill by swinging the club in one continuous motion.

You should rehearse the mechanical movements of the chip shot without a ball, simply brushing the grass with each stroke. Once you have achieved the proper technique, you can combine the walk-through movements with the correct tempo by practicing the mini-Y drill to the short-game tones. You'll soon have a properly sequenced, rhythmic chipping stroke that holds up under pressure and makes it possible to hit a wide variety of greenside shots.

———

A word about "brushing the grass." Students tend to hurry through their practice swings, paying little or no attention to whether or not they actually brush the grass. This is a serious mistake. Brushing the grass establishes the forward lean of the shaft that allows you to hit through the ball, creating crisp contact.

To be fair, many mid-to-high handicappers *can't* brush the grass due to faulty technique. They flip the clubhead with the hands, trying to help the ball into the air. That produces skulled chips, chunked chips, and the occasional shank.

So you need to take this seriously. Don't chip with an actual ball until you can consistently raise some sand and grass clippings with your practice strokes. You should *hear* the stroke, and it should have some duration, like the sound of a straight razor on a barber's strop.

Now, with the ball, try to replicate that grass-brushing stroke. You should hear a *click*—the clubface meeting the ball—followed by the sound of the leading edge raking the turf. If you hear those two sounds, you will simultaneously enjoy the *feel* of crisp, solid contact.

Frequently Asked Questions

What's the most common mistake amateurs make when chipping?

Flipping. As noted above, poor chippers try to "help" the ball into the air with the hands instead of maintaining their wrist hinge through impact. If you look at the follow-through, you'll see that the clubhead has outraced the hands, creating a dramatic cupping of the left wrist. The pros don't do that. They finish with the club and the arms forming the aforementioned 'Y', the shaft aligned with or slightly trailing the forward arm. Swinging to the correct tempo makes it easier to maintain this technically-sound position, and that's why you should practice the mini-Y drill to the tempo tones.

Aside from their mastery of tempo, do the pros employ any other chipping tricks? Something that accounts for their incredible feel around the greens?

I'd say the biggest difference between the pro and amateur chipper is that the pro invariably rehearses his shot by brushing the grass with practice swings. It's *one swing, two swings, three swings ... step back and look at the lie, look at the target ... then another swing and another, just brushing the grass.* The pro is testing the resistance of the grass, figuring out exactly how much force to apply with the club. It's like Goldilocks. *This is too hot, this is too cold, this is just right.* Johnny Miller, Tom Watson, they all say brushing the grass enhances your feel for chips. I recommend it for the full swing, as well—assuming no one is waiting on the tee behind you.

If my putting tempo is 18/9, what tempo should I use for the other short-game shots?

It's best to keep things as simple as possible, so I recommend practicing them all to 18/9.

Chapter 5

Sand Play

Most pros insist that the greenside bunker shot is the easiest shot in golf. And it is.

For a pro.

The pros demonstrate the shot's simplicity by putting on a clinic. Pro A kicks sand on his ball and then splashes it out to within a foot of the cup. Pro B *steps* on his ball, hoods his wedge, splashes it out—and pretends to be disappointed when said ball hits the flagstick and rolls a few feet away. Pro C drops *two* balls in the sand and hits both close to the hole, using only his left arm for the first swing and only his right arm for the second. If sand shots were any easier, the three pros seem to be saying, you'd have to concede them to your opponent.

What's *hard,* the same pros will tell you privately, is teaching this easy shot to an amateur. Most golfers with a mid to high handicap get up and down from sand about one time in twenty. They consider themselves lucky when the ball lands on the green and stops within comfortable two-putt range. Frightened beyond reason, they don't know if their next sand shot will roll back to their feet or imitate a baseball line drive and fly over the green.

And that's *after* a bunker lesson with a qualified teaching pro.

The pros don't give up. They point to the flange on the bottom of the wedge and show you how it creates "bounce," preventing the leading edge from digging in too deeply. They draw lines in the sand—one that leads to the target, one pointing further left along which you are to align your toes, and sometimes a third running between your legs and under the ball, a line to reveal where your club is hitting the sand. The pros ask you to fan the clubface open so that it points to the sky, and they warn you against "releasing" the clubhead through impact, because that will de-loft the club and turn your wedge into a shovel.

If you're lucky, you walk away with a tip that holds up for a round or two, something like "Slap the sand with the back of the clubhead" or "Maintain your knee flex through impact." More likely, you end the bunker lesson hitting it worse than before and more confused than ever. You drive away ill-tempered. *I did it the pro's way, and it didn't work.*

Only you *didn't* do it the pro's way. Not really.

———

Step into my editing room.

In the left window on my computer screen I have a face-on video of you hitting an explosion shot from a greenside bunker. In the right window I have a video of 2010 U.S. Open champion Graeme McDowell hitting essentially the same shot from a similar angle.

The first thing I do is time your swing. Tapping the right-arrow key to advance the video one frame at a time, I count 18 frames from the first movement of your clubhead to the top of your backswing—I make a mental note of the number—and 6 more frames back down to the point where your wedge enters the sand. I scribble "18/6" in my notebook. I repeat the process with McDowell's swing, writing down "16/8" when I'm finished.

Both swings, you will notice, consume exactly 24 frames. Congratulations! You and Graeme McDowell have identical elapsed times of .80 seconds.

You're not satisfied? You want to know why your fine shot didn't clear the lip of the bunker, while McDowell's ball hopped once on the green and dove into the hole?

Okay, let's look at the two swings in synchronized slow-motion. McDowell's backswing—which is about a foot shorter than yours, by the way—ends two frames earlier. In other words, *your* backswing takes .0666 seconds longer to complete. But don't worry, you make up the time on your forward swing. Your wedge and McDowell's wedge enter the sand at the exact same moment.

What's different is the frame ratio. Your 18/6 swing is classic Tour Tempo; it's the 3-to-1 ratio that tour pros use for their full shots. McDowell's 16/8, on the other hand, is *two*-to-1. That's the Tour Tempo that pros employ in their short games.

Now, let's think about this. McDowell doesn't take the club back as far as you do—his hands are just past waist-high when he finishes his backswing—and yet his shorter forward swing takes two more frames of video (.0666 seconds) to complete.

There's a powerful message in those numbers, but it's a message I couldn't read at first. That's because I was timing only tour players' bunker shots. What I *saw* were the numbers 7, 8 and 9 at the bottom of the tempo fractions, the same denominators that made up the bulk of the swings in *Tour Tempo*. But those were full backswings, swings where the clubshaft sometimes reached a position parallel to the ground, swings where the golfer's hands rose above his head. (See the *Tour Tempo cover photo of John Jr.'s driver swing.*) It wasn't until I started practicing with the short-game tones in a real bunker that it hit me: the sand swing is *slooooow.*

Well, duh. If two sprinters start and finish at the same time, but one runs 50 yards and the other runs 100 yards, then the guy on the short track runs much slower than his more athletic rival.

But I didn't fully get it until my inquisitive co-author started grilling me about the bunker-swing ratios of the amateurs who attended my VIP Schools. "With the full swing," Garrity reminded me, "most everyone thought the tempo tones were way too fast. Is it the same for bunker shots?"

I told him it was usually the opposite. "Amateurs think the tones are too far apart. They say, 'I can't swing that *slow.*'"

John, a mediocre bunker player at best, reacted as if one of those cartoon light bulbs had gone off over his head. Then he said, "I don't think your average golfer realizes that. When he steps into a bunker and feels all that heavy sand under his feet, he's not thinking 'finesse shot.' He's ready to grip it and rip it."

Not waiting for a response, John went straight to the million-dollar question: "Forget the frame counts for a moment. Have you compared the clubhead speeds of pros and amateurs hitting from sand?"

An awkward span of silence followed.

––––––––

This time, we started with a research population of one. Junior tested Garrity's low-clubhead-speed hypothesis by hitting a series of straightforward bunker shots (clean lie, level stance) to a flagstick 45 feet away on the Alvamar practice green using a lob wedge, an abbreviated stroke, and the 18/9 short-game tones. His SSR (Swing Speed Radar) clubhead speeds ranged from 45 to 60 mph. Junior then dropped some balls outside the bunker and hit shots with the same club, the same length swing and the same tempo toward a driving range flag up the hill. Those balls, impacted at about 50 mph, dropped to the ground about 40 to 60 yards away. Finally, Junior hit a series of full-swing lob wedges powered by his 3-to-1 long-game tempo. Those balls, launched by a clubhead speeding along at 85 to 90 mph, sailed over the target flag and landed more than a hundred yards away. "So I'm only using 50% to 60% of my swing speed for a normal bunker shot," Junior concluded.

The cartoon light bulb was now glowing over all three of our heads.

Bottom line: The shot that amateurs screw up the most is the bunker shot, and they screw it up because they think it is a power shot requiring a wide takeaway, a full turn, and a strong, fast move through the sand. The truth— and my data on tour-pro sand swings makes this perfectly clear—is that the standard sand shot is a *finesse* shot employing a partial turn, a steep takeaway and a slower-than-normal swing through impact.

Put even more simply, amateurs botch their bunker shots because they have absolutely no clue what their clubhead speed should be. They attack the sand with a full-swing tempo designed to maximize clubhead speed, when the shot actually calls for a short-game tempo that sacrifices power for distance control and accuracy.

The tempo ratio for the greenside bunker shot is 2-to-1, the same as for the putt, the chip, the pitch and the lob from long grass.

––––––––

Just as I recommend that you practice the mini-Y drill before you begin chipping to the short-game tones, I think you will benefit from a few dry runs before you take Tour Tempo into the practice bunker. You can do this at the golf course, or you can do it in your backyard—anyplace you can swing freely. Just make certain that you practice to the short-game tracks featuring the 2-to-1 tempos recommended for greenside bunker shots. (At our VIP Schools, we start our bunker instruction by having the students pitch balls onto the green from deep greenside rough. The technique and the tempo are identical to that of the bunker shot, but the grassy lie is less intimidating to the average player.)

The first step is to get familiar with the bunker tempo of the touring pros. Setting your player to 18/9, take a practice swing with your sand iron or lob wedge while listening to the tones.

- Start your backswing on the first tone, a low-pitched note.
- The second note is your cue to start swinging down to impact.
- The third note corresponds to impact. Try to time your forward swing so that "impact" and the note are simultaneous.
- Make sure that all your movements are smooth, not jerky.
- Do not anticipate the first and second tones. Just react to them with the appropriate action.

If you are like some golfers we have tested, your first impression of the short-game tones will be: "The tones are too slow. I don't think I can swing that slowly."

This is normal. You have probably been hitting sand shots with your full-swing tempo for most of your life. To you, the tour player's bunker tempo will feel like the *drip-drip* of a leaky faucet. In fact, this deliberate tempo delivers the clubhead to the sand at the reduced speed the pros employ for optimal sand play. It feels slow at first because it is slow.

Now, just to get a feel for a different 2-to-1 short-game ratio, select 20/10.

This tempo is the slowest in common use by the pros. While following the tones, practice your sand swing, checking to make sure your backswing is steeper, with more wrist cock, than your 3-to-1 power swing. As before, start the club back when you hear the low-pitched first tone; start your downswing when you hear the second note; brush the grass or sand with the club's flange on the third note.

Finally, set your player to 16/8 and make some more swings.

Remember, no matter which ratio you ultimately choose, make sure to use that same ratio for all your short-game shots. The tones establish the intrinsic tempo of the greenside shots in your subconscious mind. Once that is accomplished, you will not have to think about tempo while executing a bunker shot. It will be internalized.

As soon as you've gotten used to the tones, you will want to practice your short-game tempo in an actual greenside bunker. To aid you in your first attempts, here's my "One-Point Checklist for Successful Sand Play":

1) Practice to the tones.

Frequently Asked Questions

What about the mechanics of the sand swing? Don't you have any tips on technique?

Technique is important, yes, but conventional bunker instruction can cloud your mind. You've got your setup, your angles, your swing thoughts. *(Clubface open ... ball forward in my stance ... how much sand am I gonna take?)* That's five or six things you're thinking about, which is five or six too many. The beauty of Tour Tempo is that it takes your mind off the checklist and gets you swinging in an athletic, reflexive manner. (To learn the correct technique and tempo at the same time, I recommend that you swing our SandEasy Wedge to the tones.)

Besides, that old-fashioned technique for bunker shots may be on the way out. Some touring pros *don't* open the clubface and *don't* aim left. They don't even use a sand wedge. I see a trend toward the 60-degree lob wedge with 6 degrees of bounce. With the L-wedge, you can square up your stance and clubface and control your rollout by taking a moderate amount of sand (no spin, long roll) or just a little sand (more spin, less roll).

But for either technique to work, you have to slow down that clubhead. That's what the 2-to-1 tracks are for. (JN)

I slowed my swing down, and I still can't get out of the bunker. What now?

The two most common mechanical faults I see with amateurs are 1) too much grip pressure and 2) too wide a swing. When you grip the club tightly—which most amateurs do instinctively in anticipation of hitting the sand—the wrists go rigid, restricting your wrist cock. And that's a problem, because the explosion shot calls for an extremely narrow swing—you lift the club almost straight up with a pronounced cocking of the wrists, while simultaneously rolling the clubface open. It's nothing like the full swing, where you try to create width (for speed) as you push the clubhead away from the ball. Width with the driver is great. Width in the sand spells trouble. (JN)

Is there a drill to help me get "narrow" with my bunker swing?

There is. Place a ball on the sand near the back lip of the bunker, leaving yourself insufficient room for a conventional backswing. To hit this shot—which you occasionally encounter in a round of golf—you have to put most of your weight on your leading foot and lift the club almost straight up to avoid hitting the lip. (Remember to open the clubface on the way up.) Swinging in tempo, bring the club back down behind the ball, holding the clubface open as it skips through the sand. It will feel strange at first, but you'll be amazed at how the ball pops out and onto the green, time after time.

Once you've got the feel, hit some balls from the middle of the bunker, employing the same steep stroke. You should get the same great results. (Jr.)

I've been told to "slap the sand" with the sole of my sand wedge. Why doesn't that work for me?

Same answer as above: Your sand swing probably isn't steep enough. You aren't slapping the sand so much as raking it with the sole of your wedge—at high speed, no less. Try the back-of-the-bunker drill, and you'll finally know what it feels like to "slap the sand." (Jr.)

If I switch to a 60-degree lob wedge with 6 degrees of bounce, what do I do with my 56-degree sand wedge?

Mine is in the basement, rusting.

The Gene Sarazen-style sand wedge with the flanged sole belongs to the old bunker-shot paradigm, which has you aligned to the left and swinging across your toe line with an open clubface. That paradigm practically demands a too-fast swing, because when you lay a sand wedge open with the clubface pointing at the sky, you produce "superloft." You now need a longer, faster swing to get your ball out of the bunker. Furthermore, the old paradigm has your feet aligned one way, your clubface pointed somewhere else, and your brain trying to figure out where the ball will go.

The 60-degree, low-bounce wedge, swung at a 2-to-1 tempo, makes all those adjustments unnecessary.

Personally, I think most weekend golfers could get by with just two wedges—the 60-6 lob wedge and a 52-degree pitching wedge. I benched my gap wedge when I realized I could hit the same shots with my pitching wedge by gripping lower on the club and/or opening the clubface. Then, given the opportunity to *add* two clubs to my bag, I put in a second fairway wood and a hybrid-5. (JN)

Chapter 6

John Novosel's Little Red Book

Curb Appeal

"When I putt, all I'm doing is pitching pennies."

I use that line on my older VIP students, and they nod. But my younger students just look at me funny. What, they ask, is *pitching pennies?*

Well, it was a game that city kids—and not a few grownup hustlers—used to play. You'd stand at an agreed-upon distance from a wall or curb and take turns flicking a coin underhanded. Closest to the wall won the pot.

Couldn't be simpler, but skill was involved. Release the coin too early, and it would hit the ground. Release it too late, and it would hit the wall. That's the mechanics of pitching pennies.

The mechanics of putting aren't much different. When you let the putter face close too early, the ball rolls left. (A pull.) When you let the putter face close too late, the ball rolls right. (A push.) All you have to do to keep those two bad things from happening—assuming that your grip and setup aren't too goofy—is to get your tempo right.

That's why I say, as far as mechanics are concerned, that all you ever need to practice is a 3-foot putt.

Granted, during a round of golf you have to do your homework—figuring the break and speed, checking for grain, picking out an intermediate target. All that left brain stuff. But the stroke itself is all right brain, like a kid pitching pennies.

I'm not the only guy to see it this way. As I mentioned earlier, at a nationally-known golf school, they had us stand in the middle of the green and toss balls as close to the fringe as possible, to develop "feel."

It was pitching pennies with one difference. A Titleist or Spalding golf ball costs more than a buck.

Bunker Mentality

"Call this guy," Barney Adams told me one day. "He's 74 and still trying to figure out the golf swing."

"This Guy" turned out to be James H. Marshall, president emeritus of Hofstra University and longtime secretary of New Jersey's famed Pine Valley Golf Club. Jim had retired at about 42, and he lived in two or three houses, hosting notables like Sean Connery and Prince Andrew at his Pine Valley home. Only now he was bringing in golf gurus—David Leadbetter, Dean Reinmuth, anybody who might help him get his tee shots off the ground. Grasping at straws, he invited me and my tour-rep son to spend a few days with him at his Florida home.

So Junior and I went down to Marshall's place in Naples. It resembled the Taj Mahal. The guest bedrooms were bigger than the house I grew up in, and I was suitably impressed when Jim said my room would be occupied the following week by his buddy Tom Watson, who bunked there when he played in the ACE Group Classic. Anyway, we spent several days working on Jim's swing, getting the usual good results, and flew back to Kansas City tanned and happy.

A few months later, Jim invited us to his Pine Valley home. His tempo was fine, he said, but now he wanted to tackle a problem that had plagued him for years. "I can't get out of the sand," he said. "I blade every shot into the face of the bunker. I can't get my ball on the green." So Junior and I flew to New Jersey, where we got the same gracious reception we'd enjoyed in Florida.

Jim said, "I've got to share a story with you." It seemed that the week after we had left Naples, Jim had shared his bunker plight with his house guest,

Watson. And Watson, who is a gentleman as well as a genuine short-game guru, said, "I'll be glad to help you." Jim was a bit apprehensive because everything he had been shown by golf's best-known gurus hadn't worked.

But Watson insisted, so they went out to the practice bunker at Quail West Golf and Country Club, where the five-time British Open champ gave it his all. Watson checked out Jim's grip, critiqued his setup, briefed him on the physics of sand-wedge "bounce," shared his distance-control techniques, and drew enough lines in the sand to start a game of Tic-Tac-Toe. But nothing worked. Jim plowed up the bunker with a ton of swings, but none of his shots managed to clear the lip and get onto the green.

At the end of the lesson, Watson said, "Jim, now you've got a big problem."

"What's that?" asked the despondent golfer.

"Well, now that you've gone through the W's, the only guy left to help you is Kermit Zarley."

It's a funny story, and I tell it because it illustrates the great camaraderie and humor that golfers share with each other.

Anyway, we took Jim out to the Pine Valley practice bunker, and after a few minutes with our SandEasy club and the short-game tones, he started plopping shots on the green, one after the other. He turned to me in total amazement and said, "I've never done that in my life. Never!"

Jim Marshall passed away a few months later, after a brief illness. He was a remarkable man, a true friend of Tour Tempo, and it was our honor to have known him.

What's the bunker shot feel like?

Some years ago, my co-author came home after a week in Flint, Mich., where he'd been covering the Buick Open. "They have a nice practice bunker that's shaded by a big tree," Garrity told me, "so I hung out there during practice rounds and watched guys hit sand shots. I studied Brandel Chamblee for ten or fifteen minutes, and he looked like a farmworker tossing apples in a basket. It was all rhythm, from the way he dug his feet into the sand to the easy way he hit ball after ball up by the hole. And then Paul Azinger took his place, and Azinger was just flicking the ball up there with this flat little swing, hitting right behind the ball with an open clubface and putting so much spin on it that it came out low and stuck to the green like it was flypaper."

Garrity was enchanted by Azinger's method "because it looked so easy." And it made him ask—*Why can't I see what he's doing? Why can't I do it, too?*

I didn't have an answer at the time. Now I do. Garrity saw exactly what Azinger was *doing*, but he couldn't see the time frame in which he was doing it. Garrity was *tempo-blind*. And yet, he was right at the edge of understanding, or he wouldn't have gone on about how "easy" the shot looked. "Easy," "smooth," "effortless," "syrupy"—those words are all reliable indicators that you're in the presence of Tour Tempo.

Anyway, here's the aspect of Azinger's bunker technique that Garrity couldn't grasp.

Two to one.

Synchronized Swinging

"WOODLAND CAN THANK FAXON FOR SUCCESS"

That was the headline for a *Golfweek* article on how tour veteran Brad Faxon had helped Gary Woodland earn his first PGA tournament victory, the 2011 Transitions Championship. It seems that Gary and Brad had played a practice round together at Spyglass Hill, five weeks earlier.

It was "fascinating," Jim McCabe wrote, "the way they collaborated, especially around the greens." Faxon would pick out a spot, then he and Woodland would hit pitch shots at the same time, observing the difference in the rhythm of their strokes. "A similar drill was used with putts, as Woodland measured his speed with the putter against Faxon's."

So effective was Faxon's tempo lesson that Woodland invited him to a dinner celebration after his Transitions win.

But here, as Paul Harvey used to say, is "the rest of the story."

Woodland had turned to Faxon for help because tempo played such a huge part in his playoff loss to Johnny Vegas at the Bob Hope Classic in January. Needing merely to hit the green and two-putt on the second playoff hole, Woodland had put his approach shot in a greenside bunker. How bad was that swing? Well, it was a 28/5—way, way, way off the 3-to-1 standard for tour players.

Then, to compound the problem, Woodland put a 22/8 swing on his bunker shot (way off the short game's 2-to-1 ideal) and left himself a long putt for par.

Both players were on the green in three, but Vegas—whose tempo was 21/7 on his long shots and 14/7 around the greens—made his putt for the win.

Okay, back to Brad and Gary. Under pressure, Woodland's backswing was too slow when compared to the pace of his downswing. Ditto for his putting stroke. To solve both problems, he had played that round at Spyglass and gotten his tempos synched with those of Faxon, one of the tour's smoother operators around the greens. The payoff, little more than a month later, was Woodland's first win.

Well, that's one way to fix your tempo. But if you're like me, you won't be playing a practice round with Brad Faxon anytime soon. Fortunately, you can gain the same advantage that Woodland gained by timing your swings to the tempo of the tour pros with the short-game tones.

Feeling It

I've got another Jim Marshall story. He was worth tens of millions, having made his fortune as the owner of various enterprises, including an advertising company and an airport helicopter shuttle service. He told us that his fortunes really took off in the 1980s, a period of double-digit interest rates. But Jim had humble beginnings. He went to college on the G.I. bill and got into the securities business as a manager of mergers and acquisitions. Anything but a stereotypical tycoon, he helped found *Ms.* magazine with Gloria Steinem, co-founded the John Jacobs Golf Schools and served as senatorial campaign manager to Bobby Kennedy.

But as I mentioned, Jim's hobby was getting golf gurus to stay with him. Anybody who was nationally known, Jim would fly him in for a lesson. So before one of my visits, I told him, "Here's what we're gonna do. I'm going to write down in my notebook what I think is the most important mechanical position you should learn. And I want you to write down what *you* think is the most important position. When I get there, we'll compare notes."

So Junior and I flew into Philadelphia, where the Pine Valley van picked us up and delivered us to Jim's home. We sat down in Jim's kitchen for a drink. I opened my notebook full of tour pro pictures and showed them to Jim. He smiled and pushed a sheet of paper across the table. He'd written down exactly the same thing that all my tour pro pictures illustrated, the dynamic arrangement of club and body that the pros achieved when the clubshaft was about halfway down in the downswing—the *Delivery Zone.*

Jim understood that if you can achieve this dynamic arrangement, you can golf your ball. He knew that the pros, however different their backswings and transitions, arranged the movement of the club and their bodies in a certain order on the way down, ensuring that they would correctly release the club and attain the desired hands-ahead-of-clubhead position at impact.*

"You've read everything about the golf swing," I told him. "You've probably taken more lessons than any man alive. I bet you know as much as the average teaching pro, maybe more."

Jim nodded.

"I mean, how long have you and I been playing golf? We should be 5-under on every round, based on our years of experience."

But we weren't. That's because Jim and I—and probably you—got it backwards when we learned the game. It's not about positions, connection, Hogan's secret or the 20-point check list, and it's certainly not a question of Square-to-Square vs. Stack-and-Tilt. It's about *feel.* To play quality golf you have to learn what an efficient and powerful swing feels like, and you have to rekindle that feeling every time you play or practice.

Sam Snead, a feel player if ever there was one, put out a couple of instruction books full of the usual prescriptions and mind-numbing pointers. But Slammin' Sam recognized the hazards of the lesson tee, even for him. "Golf got complicated," he explained, "when I had to wear shoes and begin thinking about what I was doing."

Less thought ... more feeling.

Sounds like a beer commercial, but it's the proven path to better golf.

---

*Without Jim's help, I might not have come up with our new Power Tools clubs, which have changed most of my ideas about how to teach the 'mechanical' part of the golf swing. "Motion Mechanics" is what we now call that part of our program—because you learn the mechanics of the swing through feel and movement.

TOWARD A BETTER UNDERSTANDING OF TEMPO

PART TWO

Chapter 7

Dawn of a New Paradigm

It was as if someone had lit a fuse.

"TOUR TEMPO!! HOLY MOLY!!!" read the headline at *Golf Aficionados,* an online message board. Posts were popping up faster than spring tulips. "Unbelievable! ... Mind-blowing! ... Instant improvement! ... I'm firing my teaching pro! ..."

"This *Tour Tempo* book is destined to become a pivotal work," wrote GolfnutEric. "If I was a conventional instructor teaching 'right elbow here, left thumb there, turn the hips there,' I would be very worried."

"An incredible book," raved a reviewer at the 19thHole website. "After two days practice, my driver is soaring to 270 yards and is straighter! I have to change all my iron yardage by adding around 15 yards each."

KYSouthpaw79 wrote that he had "peeked at the book for a minute" at the end of work on Friday and listened to the CD on the drive home. "When I got home, I pulled out a club and started swinging to '24/8 ... Swing! ... Set/Through ...' I've always been a slow backswing guy, but the club was making a lot more noise cutting through the air than with my old swing. Saturday morning, I drove to the course listening to '24/8 ... Swing! ... Set/Through,' over and over. I couldn't get it out of my head." Normally a mid- to high-80s golfer, KYSouthpaw79 reported that he had shot 81 "with a ball in the water on number 18. And one of my playing partners called me 'smooth' a couple of times during the round. I have never been called that."

The testimonials were all over the Web. Golfers who had experienced their first "Eureka!" moment. Golfers who were suddenly reaching par-5s in two. Golfers for whom *Tour Tempo* had blown away the fog of "20-point check list" swing theories. Golfers who could suddenly hit a draw. Golfers who were repairing the damage caused by the "you'll get worse before you get better" golf schools. Golfers who had finally birdied that long par-4, the one with the inverted-saucer green.

I couldn't stop reading the testimonials, but I kept asking myself:
What'll it be like when the book reaches the stores?

———

Spring, 2004. Phil Mickelson had just won his first Masters. Tiger Woods was on the verge of firing his longtime swing coach, Butch Harmon. The last Oldsmobile was rolling off the assembly line.

The official "pub date" for *Tour Tempo* was May 10, a couple of weeks away. "That's when the book is supposed to be on shelves across the country," said the nice lady in Doubleday's New York office, adding, "But we've already shipped to Amazon."

Mystery solved! Apparently, a few struggling golfers had pre-ordered *Tour Tempo* at Amazon.com, read it on Friday night, taken it to the range the following morning, and posted 5-star reviews before *Saturday Night Live* came on. There's a term for it now—"going viral"—but I thought of it as word-of-mouth in overdrive. I checked the message boards three times a day and kept finding new threads. My favorite was "Tour Tempo Seduced My Wife!" ("I came home and found my wife in bed with the tour tempo book," complained the writer, who called himself Sir Hacksalot. "This tour tempo is out of control!") It wasn't a one-week phenomenon, either. *Tour Tempo* went on to be Amazon's top-selling sports book of 2004.

As books began to reach the stores, the traditional media kicked in. *Travel + Leisure Golf,* in a perceptive article by John Paul Newport, reported on our scoop that tour players, despite appearances, swung much faster than amateurs. "If you were to start your take-away at the same instant that a languid-swing-ing pro like David Toms started his," Newport wrote, "in all likelihood you'd still be lost somewhere in your backswing by the time Toms made contact." *Golf for Women* magazine printed a long excerpt from the book under the headline, *The Best Swing Secret No One Has Ever Told You.*

The *Kansas City Star's* Joe Posnanski, who has since moved on to *Sports Illustrated,* went so far as to liken my tempo breakthrough to the discoveries of gravity, America, and oil on the Beverly Hillbillies' land. "Tempo is one of those great words we use in sports," he wrote, "and nobody knows what it means. We just say it a lot: Ernie Els has great tempo. Fred Couples, wow, that guy's got tempo. Man, I sure wish I had Tom Watson's tempo .... But it turns out that tempo in golf is very real, it's measurable, it's something almost every single great golfer shares."

Radio and television producers, intrigued by our "Golf's Last Secret" slogan, lined up to do interviews. The best one took place at New York's Chelsea Piers Driving Range during the week of the U.S. Open, which was being played out on Long Island. John Novosel Jr. and I were signing books and giving free lessons on the fourth tier when Golf Channel's Adam Barr showed up with a video crew. Between interviews and a long-driving demonstration by Junior, Barr volunteered to try out Tour Tempo with the cameras running.

Barr's swing, a product of too many lessons, careened through several swing planes on its way to the ball. But when we put the good-humored reporter on the 27/9 tempo tones, his swing became predictably tighter, and he began slapping 7-iron shots with authority.

"It remains to be seen whether golfers of the next generation will call John Novosel golf's Edison," Barr said to the camera at the close of his piece. "For the moment, he's trying to conquer two challenges—not only the content of his instruction, but getting the idea adopted by a lot of golfers. So far, so good."

Barr's Golf Central feature ran several times that week and aired again in re-runs, spreading the Tour Tempo gospel and giving our book a significant boost.

But if I had to pick one thing that hinted at how big Tour Tempo was going to be, it would be an unsolicited e-mail that appeared in my in-box a few days after publication. Written by Hughes Norton, the retired CEO of International Management Group (and the former agent of Tiger Woods), it began, "John: *Wow! ... unbelievable! ....*"

.... I worked at IMG for 30 years, managing some of the best golfers in the world. During that time I played numerous rounds of golf with Curtis Strange, Mark O'Meara, Greg Norman, Tiger Woods, *et. al.,* each of whom tried to help me play better golf. I also had the opportunity in my job to take lessons from the top teachers in the country. Despite all this—or perhaps because of it—my golf game deteriorated over the years from a strong 4 to a current 11.

As a result of being a John Garrity/si.com fan, I bought your book yesterday and read it last night. Today at my golf club in Cleveland, I hit some of the most amazing golf shots in years. Just like the testimonials in your book, the ball is going farther, straighter, and with a little draw. As I said above, Wow! And the most amazing thing is, There Is Not One Thought of Swing Mechanics! For someone whose brain has been completely overloaded with swing correction "bandaids" for 25 years, you can't properly appreciate my joy.

You probably get a million of these e-mails, but Thank You again for liberating my swing and, equally important, my psyche from golf purgatory!

—Hughes Norton

I re-read Hughes's message many times in the weeks that followed. I couldn't imagine a stronger testimonial for my belief that golfers of all levels could improve their ball striking almost instantly through tempo training. Hughes graciously gave me permission to post his endorsement on the Tour Tempo home page, and he later flew to Kansas City for a two-day tempo workout with Team Novosel. He then capped that off with a couple-over-par performance on the Hallbrook front nine. We have become good friends.

To sum up, the first months of what my sons jokingly call the "Tour Tempo Era" were a treat. I enjoyed the attention and the favorable reviews. I rejoiced at the positive feedback from golfers who had reset their swing clocks with the Tour Tempo CD. It was a thrill to read the congratulatory e-mails from our editor, Jason Kaufman, whenever Doubleday announced a new print run. (Jason has a pretty good eye for blockbuster manuscripts. He also edited *The Da Vinci Code*.)

"The only way we could top *Tour Tempo*," I told my equally-gratified co-author, "would be by figuring out how Tour Tempo works."

Because I, uh ... didn't know.

Chapter 8

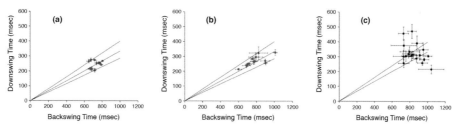

Fig. 1: A graphical representation of the tempo of the golf swing for (a) playing professionals, (b) teaching professionals and good amateurs, and (c) all other golfers.

Towards a Biomechanical Understanding of Tempo in the Golf Swing by Robert D. Grober and Jacek Cholewicki

Real Science

We all had our theories.

My explanation for the efficacy of Tour Tempo was rooted in the teachings of Ernest Jones and Percy Boomer, two of golf's seminal thinkers. Jones, a one-legged veteran of the First World War, coined the phrase "paralysis by analysis" and championed a holistic approach to golf instruction. "You can't divide the swing into parts and still have a swing," he wrote. "A cat is a cat. If you dissect it you'll have blood and guts and bones all over." Boomer, author of 1942's *On Learning Golf,* took a similar line, presenting the swing as "a connected series of feels" instead of the connected series of positions or actions taught by most pros. "Rhythm," Boomer wrote, "is the very soul of Golf."

So when students asked me how Tour Tempo worked, I told them it scrubbed the brain of the "do's and don'ts," the "swing keys," and the "20-point-checklists"— all of the faults-and-fixes bunk that inhibits breathing and restricts the golf swing. Using video of the top players, I showed my students how the pro swing was athletic and reflexive, not anxious and deliberative. I said, "Once you've internalized the intrinsic tempo in your subconscious mind, you can basically forget about mechanics. It's just instinct and timing."

That was *my* theory.

———

My co-author liked this explanation. But after watching me time a few tour players with my video editor, Garrity was struck by the *efficiency* of the pro swing. "To swing at a 3-to-1 rhythm," he observed, "you have to take the club back on a reasonably direct path, throw it into reverse at the top, and then return the clubhead to the ball without any horsing around." And by "horsing around" Garrity meant the mid-swing corrections, the loops, hitches and meanderings that weekend golfers employ in their efforts to hit the ball.

"Tour Tempo," he said, "irons the wrinkles out of a swing."

Pleased with that hypothesis, Garrity immediately offered another. Remembering how the instructors at a Golf Digest School had tried to make his swing more "connected" by strapping his arms to his torso, Garrity wondered if Tour Tempo didn't accomplish the same end without restricting his movement. "Swinging faster than I used to, my arms don't work independently of my body. Swinging 3-to-1 is a natural way to synchronize the arm swing with the body turn."

So we had *three* compelling explanations for Tour Tempo—and that was before we'd sold a single book.

––––––––

I suppose we could have consulted the experts. There are roughly 28,000 PGA of America certified teaching pros in the United States, and any one of them could have hazarded a guess as to why the game's best players swung at a 3-to-1 ratio. But they couldn't hazard that guess, I figured, until they'd read the book and learned that there *was* a 3-to-1 ratio. And having heard about Tour Tempo, there was no guarantee that either the club pros or the touring pros would accept it as fact. I had spent half the book, after all, debunking the conventional wisdom about tempo, teasing the pros for not being able to define or teach it, and decrying the "faults and fixes" paradigm of mainstream golf instruction. The teaching pros probably weren't going to be fans of Tour Tempo.

I couldn't have been more wrong.

An early hint of how the teaching fraternity would respond came in the form of an article by 2001 National Club Pro champion Wayne DeFrancesco, ranked among the nation's top teachers by *GOLF Magazine* and *Golf Digest*. "Ask 100 teachers about tempo and you will get 100 different discussions," DeFrancesco wrote, "all vague and ephemeral, using words such as 'smooth' and 'slow' and 'syrupy.' I was as guilty in my lack of precision about tempo as anybody else. That is, until —"

Until he had read *Tour Tempo,* which he found to be "an amazing revelation."

De Francesco went so far as to dig up video of his Club Pro victory so he could time his own final-round swings. He discovered that he had been swinging at a consistent 22/7. Three years later, however, having suffered from lower-back problems in the interim, he was "piddling along" at 26/8. "Thinking about my swing in terms of Novosel's discoveries," he went on, "I saw that swing length is tied closely to the amount of time you give yourself to get to the top. If I were to cut off three or four frames in the backswing, I should be able to get rid of some of the excessive movement that plagues me."

His students, DeFrancesco surmised, needed to shed even more of their unsightly swing fat. "What if I told you that every amateur swings the club back too slowly? And not by a little. I see ratios of 4-to-1, 5-to-1, even 6-to-1, and in every case the player has swing tendencies that are chronic in that they stubbornly resist change. In almost every case, when we work to speed up the swing, a transformation occurs. The swing gets tighter, more compact, and more aggressive; the comment is that it feels 'faster, but more athletic.' It might *feel* fast … but when we look at the swing on the video it never appears to *be* fast. The student is usually amazed. 'Wow, you mean I can go after it like that and I'm not breaking any laws?'"

"The next comment I hear is, 'I don't feel like I have time to think about what I'm doing.'" [*If you're keeping score, that's one vote for Garrity's de-wrinkling hypothesis and one vote for my unclutters-the-mind theory.*] "Which brings us back to mechanics."

DeFrancesco's elegant conclusion: "All mechanics exist in the framework of time; all timing exists in the framework of mechanics."

————

We also heard from a number of other club pros wanting to tell us how they were integrating tempo training into their teaching. Still more pros stopped at our booth at clinics and trade shows, eager to exchange ideas.

Garrity, our road warrior, reported from various tour stops. Calling from Rancho Mirage during the LPGA's Nabisco Championship, he described how Rob Stanger, head teaching pro at Missions Hills Country Club, used the tempo tones on his lesson tee. Calling from the press room at the Masters, he shared the fact that world-renowned swing guru David Leadbetter had just stopped him on the veranda to say that *Tour Tempo* was "a great piece of work, a real step forward." Calling from the Wachovia Championship, he held his phone next to a portable CD player on the Quail Hollow practice range and said, "Hear that?" (The familiar *beep ... beep-beep.*) "I can identify the pro practicing to your tones, but only in exchange for endorsement money."

Laughing, I told Garrity that we didn't pay pros to use Tour Tempo.

"I'm not asking for the pro," he replied. "I'm asking for me!"

———

It was gratifying to watch the tempo gospel spread around the world. A publisher in Spain put out a European version of the book. Asia's top golf teacher, Tadashi Ezure, teamed up with us on a Japanese edition. We consulted with Suunto of Finland, who, on the recommendation of Padraig Harrington, contacted us about their golf-swing-analyzing watch that provided clubhead speeds, swing times and tempo ratios for the practicing golfer. Priced at $400, it also told time.

To be sure, we heard the voices of lonely skeptics. The most interesting was A. J. Bonar, who runs a California golf school and stars in the popular "A. J. Explains It All for You" instruction videos. Bonar, almost alone among teaching pros, thought we were exaggerating the importance of tempo in golf. "I'm not criticizing," he told *Golfweek*. "I'm just wondering if the tempo by itself is the causative agent, or if other factors have come together to produce this tempo for the tour players."

It was a fair question, and I wished I had an answer for it.

But at that time, I had no way of knowing that Science had already made the turn and was in sight of the clubhouse.

———

November, 2006. That's when the Yale University study came out. Titled "Towards a Biomechanical Understanding of Tempo in the Golf Swing," it was written by Robert D. Grober, a professor of Applied Physics, and Jacek Cholewicki, a professor of Biomedical Engineering.

"It is proposed," the precis began, *"that aspects of the tempo of the golf swing can be understood in terms of a biomechanical clock. This model explains several aspects of tempo in the golf swing, the ratio of backswing to downswing time, and the relative insensitivity of tempo to the length of the golf shot. We demonstrate that this clock and the resulting tempo are defined by the rotational inertia of the body/club system and the elastic properties of the body, yielding a system which can be modeled as a simple harmonic oscillator."*

The technospeak was pretty thick, but I got the gist of it: *We're real scientists, and we're taking a look at Tour Tempo.*

I'm not being grandiose. *Tour Tempo* was cited in the very first paragraph:

> Recently, a study of the tempo of professional golfers was published in the book *Tour Tempo* [2] in which it was pointed out that the ratio of backswing to downswing time of professional golfers is of order three, $Tb/Td \approx 3$. These measurements were made using the frame rate of standard video (i.e. 30 Hz frame rate) as the clock. The tempo of the majority of tour professionals studied in *Tour Tempo* is characterized by $Tb \approx 24$ frames and $Td \approx 8$ frames. The ratio Tb/Td for all players reported in the study covered the range from 21/7 to 30/10. Also pointed out in *Tour Tempo* is that the overall tempo of professional golfers is significantly faster than that of the average golfer and that the tempo does not change significantly with the length of the shot or the type of club.

To test this provocative thesis, Grober and Cholewicki had enlisted the cooperation (and students) of three prominent golf instructors: Bill Greenleaf, PGA Master Professional and director of instruction at the Dunes of Maui Lani; Michael Hebron, PGA Master Professional and former National PGA Teacher of the Year; and David Leadbetter, founder and chief instructor of the worldwide David Leadbetter Golf Academy network. The students ranged in golfing ability from "tour professionals" and "teaching professionals" to "average weekend golfers," and their swings were timed with "motion sensing accelerometers and wireless communications electronics mounted in the shaft" with sampling rates "of order 250 Hz, yielding eight times more detail than that obtained from conventional video." Ten to twenty swings were recorded for each golfer. The club: A five-iron.

Armed with this new data, the Yale professors drew up some very cool color graphs with data points representing the average tempo ratio in milli-seconds for their three classes of golfers: a) playing professionals, b) teaching professionals and good amateurs, and c) all other golfers. Under the graphs, the authors—and here I found myself nervously reading ahead—reached the first of their conclusions:

The data for playing professionals is consistent with the data reported in *Tour Tempo*. The ratio Tb/Td varies between 2.5 and 3.5, with the average being nearer to 3.0. Additionally, these golfers exhibit very small values of standard deviation relative to all other golfers, meaning that their swings are very reproducible. Note that the time of the backswing of the tour professionals all seem to cluster in the vicinity of $Tb \approx 0.7-0.8$ sec, which corresponds to 21–24 frames per second of standard video, again consistent with the data presented in *Tour Tempo*.

As you can imagine, that paragraph triggered a small celebration at Tour Tempo headquarters. We exchanged another round of high fives over the professors' conclusion that the standard deviations measured for groups b) and c) were "much larger" than that of tour professionals.

"Additionally," continued the authors, *"the golf swings of professional golfers are universally faster than that of the average golfer."*

That one called for the Tiger Woods fist pump.

Chapter 9

Tour Tempo: The Cliffs Notes

The Yale tempo study was 16 pages long, and everything quoted in the previous chapter appeared in its first 3-½ pages. That's because validating the *Tour Tempo* hypothesis was a mere warm-up for Grober and Cholewicki. It was their L Drill with a 9-iron, to use a lesson-tee analogy. For the rest of their paper, which was devoted to the proposed "biomechanical understanding" of tempo, the professors used every club in the bag. (*Yale caddie to visiting golfer:* "The big one with the headcover is Ω. The short one with the pitted face is π.")

"In this section," the report continued, "we explore the plausibility that the simplest model of a clock, the simple harmonic oscillator, can be used to understand tempo in the golf swing of professional golfers ..."

> The simple harmonic oscillator requires a mass and a spring, i.e. a restoring force. In this proposed model the mass is comprised of the torso, legs, arms and club. The spring results from the "effective" elasticity of the biomechanical system, comprising the natural and trained response of the body. The importance of elasticity in

animal movement has long been documented ... and we propose it plays a central role in defining the tempo of the golf swing of professional golfers.

As a test of plausibility, consider the equation of motion of the driven harmonic oscillator ....

I interrupt here only because my laptop isn't loaded with the character sets required for scientific discourse—and possibly because neither I nor my co-author had a clue as to what the professors were saying once they tossed up that pinch of $cos\Omega t$ to test the wind. The English-language portions gave us a hint as to where they were headed, but it was rather like guessing where a blind tee shot will wind up.

The backswing begins with the application of a constant force ... causing the spring to compress .... The spring is maximally compressed after a period of time ... independent of the applied force. At this moment of maximum compression the position of the mass is [mathematical symbols] ... and the velocity is zero. Thus, the duration of the backswing is independent of the applied force while the maximum displacement of the backswing is proportional to the applied force .... The downswing begins at this point of maximum compression. The direction of the applied force is reversed so as to help decompress the spring and return the mass to the original position ....

I take from this the idea that a tournament pro's backswing coil, with its attendant stretching of some muscles and compression of others, functions as a non-linear spring, and springs—even biological ones—expend their force at a predetermined rate of acceleration. They do so, that is, if they are not impeded by some countervailing force—like, say, an inner voice shouting, *"Pause at the top!"*

The most efficient golf swing, in other words, is one which interferes as little as possible with this spring-like action and which operates within a consistent time frame, irrespective of the length of the shot or how much force compresses the spring. The natural frequency of this bio-mechanical spring can be expressed as a ratio of the time taken to load the spring to the time spent expending the spring's stored energy, which is—*ta-da!*—3-to-1.

Or, as we like to call it … Tour Tempo.

———

Case closed? Not quite. The authors of the Yale study admitted that the non-linearity of the golf swing posed "interesting challenges," and they conceded that their calculations were based upon "a constant applied torque and a constant rotational inertia during the backswing," when, in fact, "neither of these conditions is likely to be true." They concluded, "A complete biomechanical understanding of the tempo of the golf swing, including the non-linearity of the spring constant, the dynamics of the applied torque, and the position-dependent rotational inertia remains an open issue and is proposed as the subject of future study."

Grober and Cholewicki were smart guys. They weren't signing the scorecard until they were absolutely sure of their scores.

———

On the opposite coast, researchers at a well-funded think tank were performing their own tempo studies—the difference being that these researchers had year-round tans. I'm referring, of course, to the Titleist Performance Institute of Oceanside, Calif. Founded by PGA pro Dave Phillips and Dr. Greg Rose and operated by the Acushnet Company, TPI is the stick-and-ball equivalent of the Los Alamos labs, an R&D fitness facility where engineers, trainers and software specialists throw themselves into the essential task of squeezing three more yards out of Ben Crane's driver.

The Yale study was bedtime reading at TPI, where "biomechanical explanations" inform the training regimen. Dr. Rose describes the TPI approach as an "efficiency model," as opposed to the traditional "copy the pro" method. "If you take a hundred golfers and ask them if they'd like to swing like Tiger Woods, a hundred will say yes," Rose told *Sports Illustrated*. "But then you'll need a hundred reconstructive back surgeries."

Rose again: "There is an ideal swing for every physical capability."

To measure those capabilities and identify those swings, TPI developed a proprietary motion-capturing system. This system, housed in TPI's so-called "3-D Room," generates full-color, MRI-style sequential images of a golfer's swing. The final product looks like a cross between strobe photography and weather radar. The white shaft and clubhead fan out around the swinging golfer, whose head and torso are captured as swirls of color. The colors represent different rotational speeds—the speed of the hips, say, versus that of the shoulders.

I know all this because Tour Tempo's Director of Golf Instruction, John Novosel Jr., got to know Dave and Greg when they all gave presentations at the Swedish PGA Teaching Summit. During John Jr.'s presentation, TPI's co-founders shared their 3-D data showing that the mean tempo ratio of the tour pros in their program was 2.9-to-1. The TPI results thus confirmed the Yale study's replication of our original tempo findings.

What's more, TPI added the Tour Tempo Micro Player to its online inventory of golf-specific training aids, stating, "Tour Tempo is the only golf training aid that has been validated by an independent scientific study."

———

All right, you say, it's great that Tour Tempo has the imprimatur of America's greatest golf minds. But what about *Sweden*?

Sweden, after all, is the golfiest country in the world. More than half a million Swedes play the game (out of a population of nine million) despite a climate that puts most of its 450 courses under a blanket of snow for up to six months a year. The Swedish Golf Federation (*Svenska Golfforbundet*) is famous for its golf development programs, which have produced world-class pros like Annika Sorenstam, Liselotte Neumann, Jesper Parnevik, Henrik Stenson and Robert Karlsson. Swedish golf coaches, known for their application of psychological and sociological principles, are pursued by countries hoping to follow the "Swedish model."

The Swedes are so advanced that they were looking at tempo when Tiger Woods was still a cub. "We thought tempo was a fundamental, and we thought you should teach it to beginners," says Johan Hampf, director of education for the PGA of Sweden. "But how did you do that?"

How, indeed? The best minds in golf hadn't come up with anything better than Sam Snead's trick of swinging to a waltz rhythm or Dave Pelz's short-game mantra of *saaawish-swish*.

"We also saw that everyone playing poorly seemed to swing faster, but with no rhythm," Hampf says. "But it's so complex to get someone to perform a motor skill well. Even if you know every detail, you still have to find a way to express it to the student." America's teaching pros, similarly stymied, had decided that swing tempo was a trait, like hair color or body type. It was something you had or didn't have, not something you learned.

"The Swedish mentality is a little different," says Hampf, who was a club professional for over two decades before joining the Swedish PGA as its vice president for education. "Swedes tend to not want to stand out too much. We don't like to say, 'I'm the best.' That can be a problem in sports, but the good side of being laid back is that we're open to new ideas. We're always thinking, *I need to learn more.*"

That was Hampf's state of mind, a few years ago, when a friend lent him a copy of *Tour Tempo* that he had picked up in the States.

"There's so many books written on the technical aspects of the golf swing," Hampf says, "but only a few writers cover the softer aspects of learning. So I was excited that someone had looked into rhythm and found a way to teach it." Even better, for Hampf, was Tour Tempo's baseline simplicity. You *reacted* to the tempo tones, engaging the unconscious in the complex act of swinging the club.

"Thanks to the TPI guys, we can now measure everything so exactly," Hampf says. "That's a good thing. But too much data can be lethal in the hands of the wrong teacher. We need simple tools, like your tempo device, so we can play as unconsciously as possible."

Tour Tempo works, Hampf concludes, because it doesn't break the golf swing into component moves that have to be consciously coordinated. [*Another point for Novosel Sr., thank you.*] "I'm a fly fisherman," he says. "The feel of a good fly-fishing cast is the same as hitting a good golf shot. The flow of the river is endless. There's just the rhythm of the cast. You clear your mind, you're not thinking about anything. But as soon as you try to *force* it, to cast it far"— he gives you time to picture a fly splashing down in a tangle of fishing line—"it just breaks down."

————

So, which experts get your vote?

The scientists at Yale, who see the tour-pro swing as a bio-mechanical expression of certain laws of physics?

The trainers at Titleist Performance Institute, who use tempo as a benchmark for efficient athletic performance?

The free-thinkers of the Swedish Golf Federation, who embrace tempo training because it fits their holistic approach to golf instruction?

How about all three?

The good news, as I tell students at our Tour Tempo VIP Schools, is that you don't have to know how the 3-to-1 swing ratio works to make it work for you. All you have to do is trust it the way you trust gravity, aerodynamics, and buoyancy.

And all the other undisputed laws of nature.

Chapter 10

We're Still Learning

One of the first students who came to us after Tour Tempo hit the stores was "Guy," a retired businessman. Guy had run a company with 19,000 employees, but now he wanted to work on his golf game. "I've been to a couple of teachers," he said, "but I don't feel like I'm getting any better."

Guy's first swing had us rubbing our eyes. He took the club back slowly, and when he got to the top … nothing. His body began to lean toward the target, but the club just hung there, as if he'd snagged it on a branch. He finally threw the clubhead at the ball and hit a weak little slice.

"What do you think?" he asked. "Is it tempo?"

I was almost speechless. When we timed Guy's swing on the laptop, we got a frames ratio of 56/11. That is slooooooow. That's two-and-a-quarter seconds from takeaway to impact. By way of comparison, the average sack of an NFL quarterback occurs about 2.7 seconds after the snap of the ball. An anvil dropped from a cliff in a Roadrunner cartoon falls more than 70 feet in 2¼ seconds.

Guy's swing was probably the slowest we've ever timed. You could fit two of Rickie Fowler's 18/6 swings inside one of Guy's swings and still have 19 frames left over.

Which was great news for Guy. After 10 minutes swinging to our 27/9 tempo tones, he was hitting his 7-iron twenty yards farther and much straighter than before. Which is to say, he was now hitting a low push that flew about 125 yards. I said, "Guy, we like to work on your whole game, and I kind of notice that when you address the ball you're playing it off your right foot."

He said, "Yeah, my teacher down in Florida said if you're coming over the top it's not as bad when you play it off your right foot."

"Well, okay," I said, trying not to roll my eyes or otherwise indicate how nuts I thought this advice was, "but we're gonna' change that."

————

I tell Guy's story to make a point. When we wrote *Tour Tempo,* Garrity and I mostly relied on my data bank of professional swing times. Then, to demonstrate that Tour Tempo was an effective training tool, we conducted case studies with amateurs of varying ability, some of which we presented in the book. It was only later, as my tempo theory and products spread throughout the game, that we realized how much we still had to learn. Everything about short-game tempo, for starters—hence, this second book—but also a number of other facts, factoids and intuitions that we did not possess in 2004. Some of these discoveries derive from my continuing study of tour pro swings. Some come from my experience with students attending the Tour Tempo VIP Schools. And some came to me on a silver platter, thanks to the sharing nature of other golf educators, trainers and professionals.

A few of these nuggets are worth a few minutes of your attention.

The 5-10-15 Concept

When I first started timing pro swings, I focused on the top of the backswing. That's because the top—the point where the clubhead appeared to "freeze frame" before reversing—was the critical measuring point. At some point, however, I began to notice that tour players have almost identical takeaways, tempo-wise. When viewed from a facing-the-golfer perspective, the player's hands and/or clubshaft usually reach his pants leg in five frames. Five frames later, the clubshaft tends to be parallel to the ground. Five more frames and the shaft tends to be perpendicular to the ground.

Address　　　　　　**5**　　　　　　　　**10**　　　　　　**15**

Here's the interesting thing about this discovery: as with the all-important 3-to-1 ratio of backswing to forward swing, 5-10-15 operates independently of the pro's swing speed. The 27/9 player takes 5 frames to reach the pants-leg checkpoint, but so does his 21/7 counterpart. They're tied at the second checkpoint as well. By the third checkpoint, where the shaft is vertical, you might see a plus-or-minus-two-frame variance, but tour pro times cluster around 15 frames. This isn't a hard and fast rule, and I imagine that it will change in the future as the tour pros continue to push the 'faster tempo' envelope.

Amateur golfers, I probably don't have to tell you, don't exhibit this consistency. The takeaway of a typical weekend golfer clocks out at 10-20-25 or slower, with the occasional slowpoke taking nearly 30 frames to get the clubhead aloft. "Congratulations," I tell these amateurs, "you have mastered the 'low and slow' takeaway endorsed by most tour pros. Here's the downside: It's not the actual takeaway of a tour pro."

For the tour pros, a quick-but-smooth takeaway is second nature. That's why I now like to keep an eye on the three checkpoints. The slumping pro, in particular, seems to dawdle on the backswing. Tiger Woods, at the top of his game, was 5-10-15 on virtually every swing. Tiger Woods, as I write this, takes 11 or 12 frames to reach checkpoint two. One or two frames doesn't sound like a huge difference, but Tiger's slow takeaway throws off his natural timing and renders it less reflexive. If I were his swing doctor, I'd tell him to lose two frames and call me in the morning.

From the Ladies' Tees

Tour Tempo is a fundamental. Virtually all the tournament pros swing to the 3-to-1 ratio. I expressed it a dozen different ways in *Tour Tempo,* but I'm pretty sure I drove home the point that pros with 3.5-to-1 or 4-to-1 tempo ratios are outliers.

Did I say "outliers"? I meant "women."

When *Tour Tempo* went to press in 2004, my data base was heavily weighted in favor of modern-day PGA Tour and European Tour players, augmented by archival video of Bobby Jones, Ben Hogan, and other Hall of Fame golfers. I also timed a small sample of LPGA players to see if the 3-to-1 ratio crossed gender lines.

Annika Sorenstam, the LPGA's dominant player, timed out at a whip-fast 20/7—Tour Tempo.

Suzy Whaley, the Connecticut pro who had just become the first woman in 58 years to qualify for a PGA Tour event, timed out at 28/9—Tour Tempo.

Michelle Wie, the teenage sensation, timed out at 30/10 (spring of 2003) and 27/9 (four months later)—either way, Tour Tempo.

Se Ri Pak, the Korean star, didn't quite fit the template with her 31/9 swing, but I threw her into the rounding-error bin with two-time U.S. Open champ Payne Stewart, who was a 30/9—Tour Tempo.

Nancy Lopez, a Hall of Famer, timed out at an agonizingly slow 50/10 at the end of her career—shades of Guy!—so she was an off-the-charts outlier. Funny thing, though. When I timed Nancy's 1978 swing, the tour-rookie swing that won her nine tournaments and Player of the Year honors, I got a tidy 30/10—Tour Tempo.

And remember, the very first player I ever clocked (while editing a golf infomercial) was international LPGA star Jan Stephenson, who was a calendar-ready 27/9—Tour Tempo.

Three-to-one.

———

Fast-forward to 2011. Japan's biggest star, Ai Miyazato, has won seven LPGA events and 16 other world titles with a swing that lopes along at 50/10 five to one! Hall of Famer and 8-time-major-winner Juli Inkster, still climbing leader boards at the age of 51, hits her irons with a 4-to-1 tempo of 30/7. And get a load of Mi Hyun Kim. At 4-foot-11, she swings her driver back as far as John Daly and swings it forward as fast as Ryo Ishikawa, but she takes 8 frames longer than Daly to complete her backswing; Kim is a 32/6—*more than five to one!*

These are not popular results at Tour Tempo headquarters. Our ads lose their punch when the headline reads "Tour Tempo—the swing secret of 99% of PGA Tour pros and 62% of LPGA players."

You'll forgive me, then, if I pass the keyboard to our director of instruction, John Novosel Jr., who is better at explaining this phenomenon ....

Thanks, Dad. First of all, these slow LPGA swings are not a new phenomenon; you would have spotted the trend if you had looked at more women stars from the '70s and '80s. And had you timed more back-in-the-pack players, the women who were struggling to make a living, you would have found plenty of 4-to-1 tempo fractions. Tempos on the LPGA Tour were—and still are—slow.

Now, don't anybody get mad. This is not a put-down of female golfers.

It is just a fact that women tend to be relatively hypermobile—that is, they are on average more flexible than men. That fact alone encourages a slower tempo, because if you're hypermobile your joints just don't have any snap to them. The club goes back, your arms go up and up, your hips turn and turn ....

The second thing to consider is coaching. The prevailing dogma of the last three or so decades has been "low and slow," based upon the mistaken belief that good golfers take the club back very deliberately. Some teachers, not to be out-slowed, advocate a "pause" at the top of the swing.

So, think about it. You've got hypermobile young women, and they've been taught "low and slow." That's the perfect storm for really slow tempos. And by slow, I mean elapsed times of 1½ to 2 seconds and tempo ratios of 4-to-1 and higher.

Anyway, that's my explanation for the slow-motion swings we see on the LPGA Tour.

———

The fact that some LPGA players do not swing to the 3-to-1 ratio is somewhat surprising, but it does not undermine the Tour Tempo hypothesis. The Yale tempo study and the TPI research on tour swings demonstrate that 3-to-1 is not a personal preference; it is an expression of the most efficient application of the golfer's bio-mechanical assets. A skilled player like Ai Miyazato, in other words, would gain a significant amount of clubhead speed if she sped up to 30/10 or 27/9. That increase in clubhead speed would give her maybe twenty more yards off the tee. Which Miyazato could use. She is currently ranked 94th on the LPGA Tour in driving distance with an average of 246 yards.

This whole issue of women golfers and their tempos is really exciting, because tempo training seems to provide an immediate power boost while simultaneously improving accuracy. And "longer and straighter" is still the goal, isn't it?

I love case studies, so here's Junior again with a report from across the sea:

I presented Tour Tempo to an audience of more than 400 teaching pros at the 2008 PGA of Sweden Teaching Summit in Helsinki. On the third day of the conference, a speaker from England had to cancel due to illness, so I joined TPI co-founders Dave Phillips and Dr. Greg Rose for an impromptu breakout session on tempo. Forced to wing it, we did a hands-on with two teaching pros we pulled out of the crowd.

Our first pro's tempo was already 24/8, but he couldn't do it consistently. The next was a flexible young lady pro named Helene, who was really limber. Her backswing was crazy long, and her tempo was a draggy 34/11—Tour Tempo on Sominex. Helene was clearly athletic, and her swing fundamentals were sound. But her swing had no punch.

We were winging it, as I said, so we decided to throw Helene to the wolves. We played the 21/7 tempo track over a speaker and asked her to swing to the recording, timing her takeaway, top-of-the-swing and impact positions to the checkpoint tones. Helene laughed and feigned limpness after her first swing—21/7 must have felt like she was snatching a sausage out of a frying pan—but she quickly geared up and started whacking the SpeedBall at Annika Sorenstam's tempo.

It was amazing, the difference. Denied the time to wind her body up like the rubber band on a toy airplane, she stopped her backswing just short of parallel and powered back into the target with no observable deviation in swing plane. She still had a 90-degree shoulder turn, so the clubhead ripped through the impact zone with plenty of pop. When we played the before and after videos of Helene to the audience, you could hear a murmur of astonish-ment run through the crowd. Everyone could see how loaded and powerful she looked at the top of the backswing. It was awesome.

It was not a scientific demonstration; we didn't measure her clubhead speed. But you could really see and hear the difference. The tempo tones instantly shortened and tightened Helene's swing, allowing her to get the most out of her athleticism.

———

Subsequent testing of Tour Tempo on women amateurs of varying abilities has produced the same immediate results. In my possibly biased opinion, girls and women who are taking up the game should treat tempo as a fundamental equal in importance to grip, stance and pretending to respect a boyfriend's knowledge of the game. As for the ladies of the LPGA Tour, I hope they don't take it the wrong way when I say we need more fast women out there.

Celebs!!!

"Well, that'll be splendid. Shall we make it a shilling a hole?"

—James Bond

Who had the better tempo, Auric Goldfinger or agent 007? I'll put my money on Goldfinger, but novelist Ian Fleming was silent on the subject.

That didn't stop me from clocking the swings of Sean Connery and Gert Frobe, who played the British secret agent and his gold-obsessed rival in the 1964 movie, *Goldfinger*. Connery, who got hooked on golf during the filming, was a close-to-Tour-Tempo 29/11 despite his chicken-winging swing. Frobe, an accomplished golfer, raced through his filmed drive in 16/8—a tempo better suited for a greenside bunker shot or a tabletop laser vasectomy.

Here's another one. Bill Murray, as greenkeeper Carl Spackler, decimated a flower bed with a grass whip in the famous "Cinderella story" scene from *Caddyshack*. I timed Murray's first two swings at 48/8 and 63/6 respectively. His third effort—"It's in the hole! It's in the hole!"—was a ponderous 62/6. However, when Murray pulled off his real-life Cinderella story by winning the 2011 AT&T Pebble Beach National Pro Am with pro partner D.A Points, his tempo was a classy 30/9 for full swings and 20/10 for putting. Proof, if it was ever needed, that tempo is the key to golf fulfillment.

Why do I time celebrity golf swings? Because they're there. The PGA Tour's west coast swing offers two star-studded pro-ams, the recently-renamed Bob Hope Classic and Bing Crosby's old Pebble Beach clambake. The Golf Channel gives me a crack at additional famous hackers with shows like "Playing Lessons with the Pros," "Donald Trump's Fabulous World of Golf," and "The Haney Project."

Besides, I find it fascinating to watch extraordinarily talented people play less than extraordinary golf. Most of the celebs, as you can imagine, have tempo problems. It seems that those problems never get addressed, even though the celebrities have access to the top swing coaches in the game. At the 2011 Pebble Beach Pro-Am, comedian Tom Dreesen watched a post-Haney Ray Romano hit an errant shot and then immediately—and accurately—diagnosed Romano as a victim of Mental Checklist Syndrome. ("Ray had somewhere in the neighborhood of 137 swing thoughts as he was taking the club back.") Dreesen then hit a drive that I timed at 36/7—five-to-one!—suggesting that Dreesen's brain was just as busy.

There's nothing methodical or comprehensive about my celeb research, but here are some randomly-drawn tempo fractions for famous folks trying to hit a golf ball under trying circumstances. (Note to celebs: Tour Tempo can help you.)

Celebrity	Shot	Tempo	Comment
Ray Romano	Driver swing, early episode of Haney Project	23/9	Whoops!
Rush Limbaugh	Driver swings, early episode of Haney Project	32/8, 32/12	Limbaugh admits to "12 to 14 swing thoughts—right shoulder down, don't break the wrists …." etc.
Craig Nelson	Drive	25/8	Nice tempo
Wayne Gretzky	Iron & drive swings, PB Pro-Am	26/8 iron, 29/8 driver	Over-the-top swing

Celebrity	Shot	Tempo	Comment
Tim Finchem	Drive	25/9	PGA Commish has played some
Kelly Slater	Drive & putt at Pebble	25/9 drive, 16/7 putt	Good numbers for an am
Tony Romo	Drive and iron swing at Pebble	21/7 drive, 18/6 iron	Wow. Rock solid 3-to-1 tempo.
Charles Barkley	Late episode of Haney Project	37/10 drive, 35/8 iron	Not reactive, not athletic, casting, wanders 5 frames at top; hit it good on range, couldn't take it to the course.
Charles Barkley, left-handed	Post-Haney Project experiment	21/7	Tour Tempo! (Call a shrink!) He's not a "reflexive" 21/7, but it's awesome that he can do it left-handed
Cal Ripken	Putt	13/8	Miss
Michael Jordan	Drive & iron at Quail Hollow Championship	20/8 drive, 17/8 iron	Inconsistent tempo explains Jordan's failure to meet goals as a golfer
John Boehner	Drive	28/10	Beware the legislator with a pale left hand
Anthony Tolliver	Drive	30/6	Slow back, fast down
John Smoltz	Drive on Trump Show	22/7	Seriously good golfer with Champions Tour aspirations
Jerry Rice	Putt	18/7	Jab Miss
Kevin Costner	*Tin Cup* chips	17/7, 15/7	Inconsistent

Celebrity	Shot	Tempo	Comment
Rene Russo	*Tin Cup* driving range shot	21/9	Chicken-wing, casting swing
Don Johnson	*Tin Cup* driver swings	20/8, 21/9	Same as Rene! Good look, but loses speed into ball
Kevin Dillon	Drive on Trump Show	51/11	Entourage cancelled during backswing
Mark Wahlberg	Drive	21/7	Prize-fight training must be good for tempo
Donald Trump	Drives on Trump Series	17/8, 18/8	Short & quick … but consistent
Julius Irving	Drive at Bob Hope Classic	27/10	1 frame off a slam dunk
Jerome Bettis	Drive on Trump Show	21/8	Must have bought my book
Hank Haney	Iron shots on Haney Project	22/9, 21/8, 22/8	Consistent 2.75-to-1
Suzanne Haney (wife of Hank)	Driver swing on Haney Project	31/12	Chicken wing
Chris Berman	Drive at Pebble Beach	30/9	Perfect candidate for Power Tools club
Herm Edwards	Missed putt at Pebble Beach	16/10	"Hardest game I've ever played."
Maury Povich	Iron tee shot & 8-foot putt on par-3 at Pebble	21/8 tee shot, 12/10 putt	Great swing.
Kenny G	Same tee, iron & putt, driver on next hole	19/8 tee shot, 19/9 putt, drive 22/8	Almost identical on tee & green, unusual

Celebrity	Shot	Tempo	Comment
George Lopez	Iron at Pebble Beach	21/6	Close to Tour Tempo

Chapter 11

Playing by the Rules

Inquiring minds want to know: Are the Tour Tempo tones USGA legal?

Short answer: No.

And we're fine with that. We have never encouraged golfers to flout the Rules in any way, shape or form. The Tour Tempo tones prepare you for competition. They are not a substitute for skill. You want permission to transmit the 16/8 tones from your iPhone to your earbud when you're facing a difficult bunker shot in the finals of your club championship? Well, you won't get it here.

A more reasoned answer requires the kind of expertise you obtain at one of those Rules of Golf Workshops the USGA puts on at various sites during the first three months of the year. Or if you're pressed for time, as we are, you can simply wait for some hyper-intelligent client to do all the research for you. That's what happened to us when "Jenny"—a Tour Tempo enthusiast who had taken her handicap from 15 to 10.3 in less than a year by using the tones—asked the Royal Canadian Golf Association if it was permissible to use our tempo tones in tournaments and for handicap purposes.

"John," she wrote me, "you asked that I keep you posted re the ruling on the legality of listening to tones. Below are the backs and forths I had with the RCGA rules person."

My Question: I have recorded on a small cassette player a swing tip related to the tempo of my swing—it is simply a measured series of tones. During a round I occasionally listen to the cassette to reconfirm my swing tempo. I do not listen during my actual swing. I had assumed that this was allowed under **Decision 14-3/16** which states, "Using the device to access information on advice-related matters that were published prior to the start of the player's round (e.g., an electronic yardage book, swing tips)." Could you please confirm that my interpretation is correct?

RCGA Answer: Your interpretation is not correct. Use of such a sound is a breach of **Rule 14-3.** The types of recordings referred to in **Decision 14-3/16** relate to instruction such as voice recordings or swing thoughts (words). Listening to a sound to assist with swing tempo is using the device in a manner that directly assists the swing. *RCGA Director, Rules of Golf*

My Response: I would appreciate it if you could answer the following questions with respect to this decision, as I am now totally confused as to what the fundamental difference is between a "swing tip" (allowed on electronic media), "advice," and your ruling that a cassette tape/tones is an "artificial device" or "unusual equipment." 1. The cassette in question was never used during a swing, practice stroke or stroke. To aid my swing "directly" (defined in the dictionary as "without anyone or anything intervening, without delay or hesitation or with no time intervening"), I would have had to use the cassette during my stroke. However, there was always time intervening between my listening to the cassette and my stroke—for example, I had to turn off the cassette, put it back in my bag, select a club, step up to the tee box, go through my pre-shot routine and then make my stroke. Therefore, I would appreciate it if you could explain how you would consider that this represents direct assistance. 2. Would it be considered a breach of the rules to reference an instructional book or swing-tip book at the tee box?—for example, to verify the correct position of the hands on the club. If such a situation is considered a breach, then the rationale behind your ruling would be clear—instructional and swing tip books would also be considered as "artificial devices" or "unusual equipment." If referencing a book is permitted, however, then I can only conclude that a decision has been made to limit the use of a "swing tip" or "advice" to certain aspects of the game. In the example used, swing tips/advice related to grip are allowed, but those related to tempo are not. Could you please comment on the preceding and explain why one is allowed and not the other? I really am struggling to understand why using a book to promote a mental image of the right grip should be considered differently than using a cassette (or caddie's advice) to promote a mental image of the right tempo. 3. The Rules allow my caddy to give me advice. Advice has been defined as any counsel or suggestion that could influence a player in determining his play, the choice of a club or the method of making a stroke. Is my caddy allowed to give me advice on the tempo of my swing? For example, could my caddy drum out with his hands the tempo, verbalize the correct tempo or simply parrot the tones contained on the cassette before I take my stance and stroke? Finally, 4. I wonder if you could give me some specific example of acceptable audio-tape swing tips as per **Decision 14-3/16.** Thank you very much for your patience in this matter. Respectfully submitted, Jenny.

RCGA Answer: The Joint Rules Committee of the R&A and USGA have determined that listening to a sound as you describe directly assists the player with the tempo of their swing and is therefore not permitted. Other instructional recording, such as spoken words—like a recording of an instructional manual—only provide guidance to the player. The player still must execute on the advice. It may be a subtle difference, but one that the world governing bodies have made. 2. Referencing an instructional manual is permitted for the same reasoning as above. Your interpretation is not quite accurate. If a swing tip on tempo were an instructional tip, versus an actual sound of a tone, then it would be permitted. The player would still have to create the tempo in their mind. 3. Your caddie may provide any kind of advice they wish, except as restricted by **Rule 14-2.** Again, the caddie would have to create it; it could not be a recorded tone. 4. Specific tips would be any spoken words recorded before the round. The intention of the decision is to permit a recording of swing tips in addition to the written version.

My Rejoinder: Thank you for your response re my questions re the ruling on listening to tones. From the timing of your Email, it appears that you are working night and day. You are indeed correct in your statement that the difference is subtle. To summarize my understanding, it is legal for me to follow directions in a book showing me precisely where to place my hands on the club; indeed, I could keep my hands in the instructed position and then take my stroke. This is legal because the book is classed as guidance that I must interpret and upon which I must execute. Contrarily, it is not legal for me to listen to three tones on a cassette, to then interpret how I must apply them to the component parts of my swing (which indeed I must do) and then try to execute on this interpretation when I eventually make my stroke: This is deemed to "directly" assist my stroke. With all due respect to the Rules decision bodies, the logic of this is elusive, and I would hope that you might pass this on in the hopes that they might try to better explain their rationale. One final question (and then I'll stop bugging you on this one). You stated that "if a swing tip on tempo were an instructional tip versus an actual sound of a tone then it would be permitted" and that "specific tips would be any spoken words recorded before the round." Would I be correct in assuming, then, that any series of recorded spoken words that reflected a swing tempo (for example, a musical piece or simply just a phrase spoken with the rhythm I want to use) would also constitute a breach of the rules? If this is the case, then shouldn't this be reflected in the rules or decisions somewhere so that players cannot cheat and receive what has been deemed to be direct assistance? If this is not the case and players may listen to music or "non-tone" renditions reflective of their chosen tempo, then the entire point of this particular ruling becomes rather moot. Respectfully submitted, Jenny.

RCGA: Hi, Jenny, Sorry for the delay. I am at a competition this week. The Decisions are updated every two years, and this particular topic has only recently been discussed. Listening to music has been permitted based on the understanding that its use is not directly assisting the swing. While you may have brought up a grey area in this regard, the fact remains that the rules makers have deemed listening to sounds for the specific purpose of assisting the player in her swing to be a breach. I'm afraid I cannot shed any more light on this issue. Sometimes one must accept a rule or decision at face value, regardless of whether it makes sense to one. I can assure you that a great deal of thought goes into every rule and decision.

––––––––

"Bottom line," the wonderful Jenny wrote, "is that the tones are illegal."

Chapter 12

Tempo FAQs

Can I develop good tempo just by watching golfers with good tempo?

The best evidence that you *can* absorb good tempo through your eyes is anecdotal, and it comes from the pros themselves. "I picked it up when I was a kid by watching my dad," one pro will say. Another will claim to have found his groove while caddying for a club pro "who knew Hogan." None of these tales, however, offers hope to a sedentary 20-handicapper with a figure-8 backswing.

The bigger problem is that swing timing is hard to judge with the naked eye. Ernie Els looks like he's swinging slowly, but he's actually whipping his clubhead into the ball at 110 mph. Tommy "Two Gloves" Gainey, meanwhile, seems to race through impact as if somebody has fired a shotgun behind him. The eye registers their swings as *smooth* (Els) or *jerky* (Gainey), but those are attributes that apply to their good swings and bad swings alike.

Hey, if simply watching was the answer, we'd all have great tempo from the hours we've spent watching the pros on TV. (JN)

Can I screw up my tempo by watching golfers with bad tempo?

I'd probably say yes. Some pro-level data suggests that golfers with dissimilar tempos can influence each other during a round, to the point that some pros avert their eyes when the other player swings. It follows that an amateur with shaky timing will suffer in the company of a golfer with a glacially-slow backswing or a downswing that resembles a snapping mousetrap.

The pro move is to search the sky for jet contrails while the guy with toxic tempo hits his shot. (JN)

27/9 felt really fast when I first tried the tones, but now it feels normal. Should I try 24/8 now? Or 21/7?

That's exactly how I felt when I discovered Tour Tempo. The answer is, you might be rewarded with longer and straighter shots if you quicken your tempo even more, but there's no data to support that. But, by all means, give it a try. Use whatever tempo gives you dependably good results. *Consistency* is the holy grail of tempo training. (JN)

I'm a 24/8. What's my elapsed time?

We get this question a lot, and the math is pretty simple. Take the total number of video frames in your tempo ratio—in this case, 24 + 8 = 32—and multiply it by 0.033 seconds, the time between successive frames of video. A 24/8 swing takes 1.06 seconds from takeaway to impact. A 16/8 putt rounds off to 0.8 seconds. (JN)

How do I take my "range swing" to the course?

By developing a consistent pre-shot routine. Tour players rarely hit a full shot, in practice or play, without going through a routine that gets them into the correct rhythm. You should follow their example.

By the way, I can invariably tell the handicap of a player by watching his or her pre-shot routine. A consistent pre-shot routine usually translates into consistent play on the course. Standing over the ball for minutes going thru the 20-point checklist, not so much. (JN)

Is there a tempo component to a good pre-shot routine?

For sure. If you pick out a target, approach the ball, and settle into your stance the same way on every shot, you're more likely to develop a rhythmic sequence that carries through impact and into a balanced follow through. When practicing, for example, *try synchronizing your pre-shot routine to the tempo tones.* Place the clubhead behind the ball on the first beat ("Swing!"), then position your feet on the next two prompts ("Set! Through!"). You can then execute your club waggles to a cycle of the tones before drawing the club back for real.

The pre-shot routine is thoroughly explained in the CD that comes with our original book and in the iPhone apps in the video section (under "Workout"). It's 5 minutes and 41 seconds into that video. (JN)

My swing seems to speed up when I'm under pressure. Any advice?

Your too-fast-under-pressure swing is probably a short swing. When your muscles tighten up, it gets difficult to complete the backswing. You'd be well advised to take a deep breath or two, which will send oxygen coursing through your bloodstream, helping your muscles relax.

But again, it's your pre-shot routine that helps you with any make-or-break shot.

Let's say you're in a four-ball match. (Think Ryder Cup or your club's member-guest.) And let's say your partner has just dumped it in the water on a forced-carry par 3. It's totally up to you to win the hole.

That's a lot of pressure to put on your swing. That's why, at this point, you just want to go through a process. First, perform all your left-brain calculations—yardage, wind, choice of club, etc. Once that's done, just step up to the ball and go through your pre-shot routine.

At that point, you have to "Man Up" and accept what happens. (JN)

———

The tour pros take their pre-shot routines seriously, but they're still susceptible to pressure. The difference is, the pros tend to get slow when the heat is on, not fast. Playing the 72nd hole with a one-stroke lead, the tour player sees water on the left and a pot bunker guarding the pin (and, with his mind's eye, the million-dollar winner's check), and he tells himself, *Smooooooth … Keep it slow … Don't jump at it … Give it just 90% … Stay within yourself.* If he subdues his adrenaline rush, he knocks it stiff and collects the big check. If he dials it back *too* much, he's Greg Norman blowing a six-stroke Sunday lead at the 1996 Masters.

Personally, I think most pros, when they talk about speeding up under pressure, aren't really talking about their swings. It's their thinking that gets rushed. When the pro feels stress, he gets impatient, he makes mistakes. He forgets to check the wind. He misreads his yardage book. He pulls the wrong wedge. He may then hit his shot with perfect tempo—those guys are good—but his ball may still wind up in the pot bunker. (Jr.)

Should I be thinking of the tones in my head when I'm playing a round of golf?

I wouldn't normally recommend it, but our motto is "if it works, then do it." I think tempo training establishes the *feel* of the swing, and it's that *feel* you should be trying to replicate during a round, not your possibly-innacurate memory of the tones. (JN)

———

I'm with my dad on this one. When you use the tones on the range (or while hitting your SpeedBall at home), you're "grooving" Tour Tempo. You should be able to take that tempo to the course. (Jr.)

———

May I offer a spirited dissent? I'm one of the Novosels' original satisfied customers—Tour Tempo got me off the mats and back out on the golf course—and I *never* hit a ball without mentally reciting some variation of the tones. I'm thinking *beep … beep-beep* or *"Swing! … Set! Through!"* as I start my pre-shot routine, and I keep the mantra running in my head until the ultimate *beep* of impact. I concede that my head tones may not match the 24/8 I practice to, but they prepare me for a 3-to-1 swing almost as effectively as the real tones do.

John points out that many golfers will not have my "ear." I'm a semi-pro guitarist and an amateur jazz pianist, so I process Tour Tempo like a studio drummer following a click track. I hear the tones as a measure of 4/4 time with the beeps on beats 1, 3 and 4, followed by a full measure of rest during which I count the beats. ("One-two-three-four ….") This, I remind John, is precisely what the musicians did on his "Tour Tempo Tracks" music CDs. Those songs, with included human reaction time, train you to swing to a 3-to-1 ratio in 4/4 time.

The head tones may not work for everyone, but they work for me. John Jr. timed me surreptitiously during a recent round—I was hitting an 8-iron on a par 3—and showed me the iPad video when I walked off the tee. "You were 24/8," he said. "Perfect Tour Tempo."

They're right, it's about *feel*. But rhythm and feel are soul mates. (JG)

How does Tour Tempo relate to swing speed? In other words, if I have the same downswing frame count as Keegan Bradley, will I have the same clubhead speed?

We haven't established a perfect correlation between elapsed swing time and clubhead speed. A 6-frame downswing might produce a 120-mph CHS, or it might produce a 90-mph CHS. So, no. Even if you have the same downswing frame count as a tour pro, you won't necessarily match his 112-mph swing speed. (PGA Tour average.)

Junior explains it this way: "Imagine a one-mile car race. Car A gets off to a super-fast start and takes a big lead, while Car B starts slow but keeps accelerating. Car B gradually catches up, and the two cars cross the finish line together (same elapsed time). But while Car A is going 100 mph, Car B is going 130."

It's the same with tournament golfers. They keep the clubhead accelerating through impact, while most amateurs reach peak velocity *before* impact. Same elapsed time, but vastly different clubhead speeds.

That said, you *will* probably hit the ball farther if you speed up your swing—assuming the length of your swing remains constant.

If you start at more than 30/10 and increase your tempo to 24/8 or less, you might see a 5-to-15 mph increase in clubhead speed. That could gain you ten to thirty yards off the tee.

If your tempo is 27/12 from casting—casting costs you frames on the downswing—and you speed up to 27/9, you'll gain the same ten to thirty yards. This scenario applies to most average golfers.

If you go from 27/9 to 21/7, there's a good chance you'll be hitting it ten to twenty yards farther. That's typical for the better-than-average golfer who thought he was *supposed* to go slow.

If you go from 24/8 to 21/7, same result. More distance. (JN)

———

Our poster boy for speeding up your tempo was in the original book. Bruce Provo went from 44/11 to 31/10 and began hitting his driver 40 yards farther and his irons 25 yards farther.

So you're wondering: *He only sped up his downswing by one frame, and he gained all that distance?*

The explanation lies in the race car analogy. Bruce got back to impact faster *and with more acceleration.* That's a powerful combination. Notice, as well, that his new tempo matched Tour Tempo. As a result, he became race car B. His more reflexive, athletic swing made his clubhead speed much faster at impact. He went from 90 mph to 107 mph in less than an hour. (Jr.)

How long will it take me to get that promised increase in clubhead speed?

I'll let Jim Achenbach answer this one. Jim is *Golfweek*'s equipment and technology editor, and in October of 2004 he wrote an article titled "My Need for Speed."

"My quest started five or six years ago," he wrote, explaining how he had never been able to achieve his goal of 100 mph of clubhead speed, 97 mph being his measured best. "To put this in perspective, consider that any touring pro under 110 mph is considered a wimp. Many are faster than 120. Some of the stars of the Long Drivers of America circuit are able to approach 150."

Jim used the word "humiliating" to describe his futile pursuit of power. "I played with Annika Sorenstam; she outhit me by 30 yards. I played with Michelle Wie; she outhit me by 40 yards. (I decided to stay away from Laura Davies.) My friends laughed at me. I was the guy who couldn't keep up with the girls. I thought about changing my name from Jim to Janice.

I talked with hundreds of golf instructors, some of them famous and highly paid. I took lessons from dozens of them. They all remarked on my smooth swing. However, waiting for my swing to reach 100 mph became something like waiting for the second coming of Bobby Jones. I had to admit the truth: It wasn't gonna happen."

And then he heard about Tour Tempo from a reader … and decided to spend three days in Kansas with us at one of our VIP Schools. "We started at a practice range," he reported.

> We measured my swing speed with a 5-iron and a driver. There were no surprises. I made a dozen driver swings, and every one was between 93 and 96 mph.

> Before I scream with jubilation, let me fast-forward to the end of the day. After several hours of classroom discussion and drills, we returned to the range. Same driver, same measuring device: All my swings fell between 102 and 106 mph. My slowest swing topped the 100 mph barrier, and my fastest swing was 10 mph faster than it had been in the morning.

> When I viewed a video tape, my swing didn't appear to be nearly as fast as it felt. And my increased swing speed was proof that something positive was happening.

> I bought dinner. Drinks were on me. I might not change my name to Janice.

The increase in clubhead speed, as Jim discovered, is immediate. What's more, Tour Tempo also enhances the other part of the long-hitting equation— the quality of your hits. The squarer you strike the ball, the farther and straighter it goes.

With no waiting.

Can I Time My Own Swings?

You can, and you should. All you need is a video of your swing, a computer, and a digital video player with stop-frame capabilities. Any editing program will have a *frame counter* and a *time tracker*. Note the frame (A) where the clubhead first begins to move on the swing-away, the frame (B) where the clubhead comes into clear focus at the top of the swing, and the frame (C) that captures impact with the ball. Subtracting A from B gives you your tempo numerator. C minus B gives you your tempo denominator.

But that's doing it the hard way. I simply open the swing video in QuickTime Player on my Mac. Then, using the right arrow key, I literally count the key strokes from takeaway to the top ("… twenty-four, twenty-five, twenty-six …") and from the top back down to impact ("… four, five, six …"). It's that easy.

We are currently working on a frame counter app for the iPhone so that you can track your tempo on the go. (JN)

I can do the Y drill great when I'm just brushing the grass, but with a real ball I get that "hit" impulse and lose my timing. Any suggestions?

When I see people messing up the drills, it's because they don't have any awareness of how far back they're taking the club. I'll say, "Do a Y drill," and they give me an L drill. When I say, "Do an L drill," they make a full swing. It's because they're trying to hit the ball too far.

To make that point, I ask the student to hit the ball fifteen yards with a 9-iron. The student typically chips the ball ten or fifteen yards. No problem. But when I ask the same student to hit a ball with the Y drill swing, he hits it *fifty* yards. He uses way too much swing. (Jr.)

When I do the Y and L drills, I can't seem to stop the club where John Junior does. And if I do stop it there, it causes me to decelerate into impact. We don't want that, do we?

Actually, we do want you to decelerate—but *after* impact, not before. But first, answer this question: *Are you really doing a Y drill?* You may be taking a fuller backswing than you think. If your swing length checks out, look at how hard you're swinging. Almost everyone tries to hit these less-than-full shots too hard.

If you're making the proper length swing with the proper force, you should find it easier to get the same finish as Junior and the tour pros. But if you're still having problems, it's because you're using your hands and arms to make the motion. You have to coordinate your body turn with the motion of your hands and arms; otherwise, you'll "cast" and/or "flip" the club. (Casting means you're uncocking your wrists too early in the downswing. Flipping is a sudden unhinging of the trailing wrist through impact in a misguided effort to gain power or to lift the ball into the air.) A good rule of thumb with the Y drill is that you should maintain "trail wrist extension." If you're right-handed, that means you should see wrinkles on the back of your right wrist at impact.

The other related issue is what I call "help." Amateurs instinctively try to deliver a last-instant hit to the ball, usually with the trailing hand. Unfortunately, when you add help to the club, you lose command of it through impact. You have no way of controlling the ball's trajectory or spin.

As for the second part of your question, we want you to *accelerate* through impact and then quickly *decelerate*. Every pro we've clocked can do this. That's how they hit those precise pitch shots and those wind-cheating knockdown shots. Their secret? The pros use their *bodies* to stop the club's forward motion. If you're still baffled by deceleration, it's because you're not maintaining the Y of your arms and body as you make your turn. You're swinging with your hands and arms alone. (Jr.)

———

All of the above having been said, the easiest way to 'feel' the proper swing sequence is by using our new Power Tools Pitching Wedge club with the "Power Drill." (JN)

I've been having great success with the Y and L drills and the Tour Tempo tones. Do I continue doing the Tour Tempo Workout indefinitely? Are there other drills I can incorporate?

The drills are great, and yes, you need to keep doing them. I liken it to eating and exercising. If you're feeling great and looking great due to a good diet and exercise program, you need to continue those practices to maintain those results. Same thing with your golf game. The more you do the Workout to keep your swing in tune, the better it will serve you.

Furthermore, you should analyze your game to determine what other drills, exercises or stretches you might need. Then ask yourself what you can do to turn your weaknesses into strengths. Similarly, you can overcome a sedentary lifestyle with golf-specific stretches and exercises. Is it your mind that needs expanding? Coaches and behavioral scientists are finding new ways to unlock your golfing potential. I should add, in passing, that I'm putting together a Tour Tempo book that will address all of these areas. (Jr.)

Is there anything else out there, besides counting frames, that can measure my short-game tempo?

Technology marches on. In June of 2011, Ping released a putting app for the iPhone/iPod that claims to measure several parameters of your putting stroke, including tempo (expressed as plus or minus the desired 2-to-1 ratio). The iPING app is free, but you need to buy a plastic cradle for the iPhone, which clips to your putter shaft. We were still testing iPING's accuracy as we went to print.

For a complete rundown on our own product line, which includes the new and revolutionary Power Tools training club, check out the "Bag Room" section at the end of this book. (JN)

THE PRO-SPECTIVE ON TEMPO

ON TEMPO

PART THREE

Chapter 13

Proamble

Sometimes, on a spring or summer afternoon, my iPhone rings. I drag it out of my pocket and check the caller I.D. If it reads *Garrity, John*, the conversation goes something like this:

"Hey, Tempo King, how ya' doin'? Have I caught you at a bad time?"

There's usually a buzz of conversation in the background, or the sound of canvas flapping on metal poles.

"No. What's happening?"

"Well, I'm in the press room at Pebble, and Dustin Johnson just coughed up his overnight lead with a triple-bogey on the second hole—you're watching, right?—and now he's tried to drive the green on No. 3, and he's hit his ball so far left that they've got guys in pith helmets and jodhpurs looking for it ...."

Laughing, I lean my Electric Putter against the wall. Then, with the phone still pressed to my ear, I start up the carpeted stairs to my attic studio.

Sometimes the call comes from halfway around the world. From Dubai. From Auckland. From Versailles. Wherever it's from, I know where it's leading.

"Greetings from St. Andrews! I hope I didn't wake you, but I thought you might be running the numbers on our boy, Louie."

"I just turned it on."

"You know, I thought Oosthuizen would lose his nerve, but he's hitting every fairway and he's putting like it's a practice round. So I was wondering if you could fire up the frame counter …."

The calls are an enjoyable but unintended consequence of my collaboration with Garrity on *Tour Tempo*. When John interviewed me for the book, I demonstrated my frame-counting technique using freshly-recorded tournament videos. I'd say, "Here's Steve Stricker on the third tee at the Memorial, a perfect 24/8." Or, "This is Lee Westwood in the fairway at Troon—22/7, and the ball releases up to the hole." I cued up dozens of swings to prove that Tour Tempo was measurable and that it was a predictable 3-to-1 ratio of backswing to forward strike for all the top players.

John thought the evidence was strong, but the swings that interested him most were those that did *not* conform to the theory. "What was *that*?" he asked, watching Phil Mickelson slice two drives into the barranca on a playoff hole at the 2001 Buick Invitational at Torrey Pines. When I told him that Mickelson's wild shots were the product of wayward tempo—28/8 and 29/8, respectively—John peppered me with questions. "Is he consciously slowing his backswing? Is he taking the club further back? Does he lose his spine angle?"

I explained that a tour player typically hits a bad shot because of a too-slow takeaway or because he feels out of position at the top and wants to "save" his swing by rerouting the club. Mickelson's tempo-killing move was easy to spot. When I advanced the video frame by frame, the change of direction at the top of his swing consumed three frames instead of the usual one. The butt of the club, instead of going directly down to impact, moved a few inches behind him—a hitch—before starting down.

John had his own word for this kind of top-of-the-swing adjustment: *dithering*. "I can't see it at normal speed," he said, "but the effect on the shot is incredible."

When I showed John more examples of tour players hitting their worst shots—snap hooks, shanks, skied drives, fatted and thinned irons—he had another question. "Did you time these swings because the shot was bad?" Before I could answer, he waved me off. "No, let me ask it this way. If you look at random video of pro swings, can you guess the outcome of the shots from the frame count alone?"

My answer: "Yeah, pretty much."

———

I don't want to overstate my powers. I can't predict that an iron hit with perfect tempo will land safely on the island-green seventeenth at the TPC of Sawgrass. The pro might have mis-clubbed, or the wind could have shifted. But when I clock a tournament swing that is off by several frames, my diagnosis of "bad shot" is usually confirmed by the pro's body English and his pained expression. Or he drops the club before completing his follow-through. The latter is often accompanied by a shouted profanity, but the verdict is in before the cussing reaches my ears.

Anyway, John reacted to my claim by drawing a big star and three exclamation points in the border of his notebook. "This is great," he said. "You've found a new way to analyze swings without the consent of the players."

Golf reporters, John went on to explain, while "extremely bright and articulate," are not actually golf experts. Knowing this, tour players routinely brush off their questions about a bad round by saying "I was fighting a pull" or "I keep getting stuck" or some other variation of *You wouldn't understand.* Reporters waste even more time indulging superstars who insist that their swing changes are very close to paying off despite their current propensity for sculling approach shots and driving into water hazards. "For swing analysis," John said, "we've got TV gurus like Johnny Miller and Peter Kostis, and they're terrific at pointing out things like head movement and swing plane. But they don't know what tempo is, much less how to fix it."

After the book came out, Garrity told interviewers that he expected the "tempo fraction" to become a data point for television, print and online analysts. "You'll have a little window on the screen that shows how Vijay's last swing clocked at 24/10 instead of his tournament winning 24/8, and that's why his ball flew out of bounds. Then Miller can use the telestrator to show how Vijay's slow downswing threw him off."

I'm still waiting for that prediction to come true, but John was certainly right about Tour Tempo's potential value to journalists, swing doctors and anyone else—gamblers?—wanting to know how tour players are really swinging. For that reason, I continue to record tournament telecasts for the express purpose of timing professional and amateur swings.

Do I time everybody? No. It takes me about five minutes to cue up a swing, accurately tag the three points of measurement *(first move away from the ball, change of direction at the top of the backswing,* and *impact),* count the frames and enter the data on a digital spreadsheet. I'd be overwhelmed if I attempted to do that for every player in a 144-man PGA Tour field.

Do I time every one of a chosen player's swings? Again, no, and for the same reason. Assuming I'm lucky enough to pick David Duval the day he shoots 59 to win the 1999 Bob Hope Chrysler Classic, that's still 59 swings × 5 minutes = 295 minutes. And that's not allowing for coffee breaks.

Instead, I time a few players at each event.

First, I clock the phenoms—kids like Rory McIlroy and Ryo Ishikawa—to establish a benchmark I can use to track their evolution as players. That's how I know that Michelle Wie was a 30/10 at the age of 14, a 27/9 when she was 15, and a 24/8 when she won her first LPGA event at the age of 20.

Then I clock the stars, fan favorites like Tiger Woods and Phil Mickelson. I time the top players for the same reason that auto mechanics run diagnostic tests on engines—to see how they're running. That way, when the announcer says, "Tiger must have misread that putt," I can prove him wrong by showing that Tiger's stroke was a jabby 14/6 instead of his usual 16/8.

Finally, I clock the guys on the leader board. I time the frontrunners because, as Willie Sutton might have said, "That's where the good tempo is"—but also, I admit, because TV mostly follows the leaders. (I need an unobstructed view to accurately track a clubhead from takeaway to impact.) By scrutinizing early final-round video from the 2010 U.S. Open, for instance, I found that Graeme McDowell's 21/7 swing was purring like a finely-tuned Bentley, while third-round leader Dustin Johnson's 21/7 was leaking oil before he even left the range.

I'm ten years into this fool's errand, and guess what? I've got hundreds of megabytes of tempo data covering practically every tournament pro who has ever swung in front of a TV camera. This information is priceless.

Did I say priceless? I meant worthless.

The truth is, any pro who wants to know what his tempo used to be can dig out an old video and count the frames himself. Journalists can do the same—although, as Garrity points out, it's far easier to call "that guy in Kansas" to find out why Ian Baker-Finch's game went south. Maybe someday I'll establish a consultancy and provide fee-based tempo data to the networks or the golf tours. But for now, timing pro swings is simply my hobby.

That said, if you'd like to know what my research reveals about the pro game and certain famous golfers ... turn the page.

Chapter 14

General Observations

Let's begin with our most significant finding: *Tournament pros swing faster than they did a decade ago.* No, check that. The typical world-class golfer of 2011 swings faster than his counterpart of 2005. That's only a *half* decade ago.

This boggles my mind.

Conventional wisdom says that *technology* has transformed golf in the last couple of decades, that improvements in club design and ball composition account for the 300-plus-yards driving averages and the record scores at tournaments. Titanium clubheads, graphite shafts and urethane mantles explain the rounds of 59 or better shot by an LPGA legend (Annika Sorenstam), a journeyman pro (Paul Goydos), a former Australian Rules football player (Stuart Appleby) and a Japanese teenager (Ryo Ishikawa).

I'm not saying the conventional wisdom is wrong; independent testing confirms the longer-and-straighter properties of contemporary golf gear. But my tempo data suggests that there may be one or more other variables influencing tour performance.

Here are some numbers to chew on:

When I began timing tour swings in 2000, roughly 95% of the players were covered by the three most common elapsed times and frame ratios—27/9,

24/8 and 21/7. They all had the same tempo—a roughly 3-to-1 ratio of back-swing to forward swing—but they could be categorized as fast-swinging 27/9s (Jim Furyk), faster-swinging 24/8s (Steve Stricker) and really-fast-swinging 21/7s (Matt Gogel). A handful of tour players (Payne Stewart, Jay Haas, Se Ri Pak) were weekend-golfer slow, meaning that they had backswing frame counts of 30 or higher. But no pro was "freaky fast." The only active tour player with a consistent takeaway-to-impact time of less than 27 frames was Fulton Allem (19/7).

Furthermore, the frequency distribution for tour swings was pretty much equal for the three most common elapsed times, as it had been since the days of Gene Sarazen and Walter Hagen. That is, there were about as many 27/9s chasing Tiger, Phil and Vijay as there were 24/8s and 21/7s. A golfer's elapsed swing time, I inferred from the data, was arbitrary and personal. It was the golfer's ability to consistently swing at the 3-to-1 "tour tempo" that made him play like a pro.

But now, in 2011, a distribution curve of PGA Tour and European Tour tempos shows a veritable stampede toward the uptempo end of the graph. The 27/9-and-slower demographic now represents a smaller fraction of the whole, while the 21/7 and 24/8 groups represent a strong majority. Tellingly, there are now a number of players who are freaky-fast, including Young Guns Rickie Fowler (18/6), Rory McIlroy (19/6 in 2010) and Matteo Manassero, 18/6. And if you think *they're* fast, you haven't seen 22-year-old John Peterson, who won the 2011 NCAA individual championship and then, still playing as an amateur, finished second in the Nationwide Tour's Children's Hospital Invitational with a fastest-we've-seen 16/5 swing.

The fact that the freaky-fast players tend to be very young suggests that the movement to faster swings is *generational*. The phenoms are earning their tour cards with lightning-strike drives and trip-wire iron shots, and they swing that way because they are strong, they are flexible and they are cocky. If you were drafting them for an NFL team, you would play them at safety or wide receiver.

But hold on. When I compare the current swings of veteran tour pros to the 2005 swings of the same pros, I find that the 30-and-40-somethings—who are *not* stronger, more flexible and cockier than they were a half-decade ago—are also gravitating toward faster swings. Phil Mickelson, once a deliberate 27/9, is now a 24/8. Padraig Harrington has cut .23 seconds off his 25/8 swing and can now race the ghost of Ben Hogan to the ball with .0333 seconds to spare. Tiger Woods is now so fast that his clubhead often meets the ball before the Tiger of 2000 has finished his backswing.

These numbers are a hammer blow to the old paradigm, the theory that a golfer's tempo is determined by his temperament. The high-strung, impatient fellow, we were told, talks fast, walks fast, and lashes at the ball like Arnold Palmer (20/7), while the smiling, easy-going guy whistles while he walks, stops to smell the roses, and swats the ball like 57-year-old Jay Haas (30/10). But if that's true, what accounts for successful tour pros whittling as much as a quarter of a second off their swing times? They surely haven't spontaneously become type-A personalities.

There are a couple of plausible explanations. The first, favored by your friendly neighborhood swing coach, cites the well-established trend of long-hitting tour pros shortening their swings and simplifying their mechanics to, as they say, "reach the next level." Davis Love III fits the model. Awesomely long but not always straight when he burst onto the Tour in the late '80s, Love snipped a foot or two of clubhead travel off his driver swing in a bid to hit more fairways. The change did him good; he won 16 tournaments and made every U.S. Ryder Cup and Presidents Cup team between 1992 and 2003. It also saved Love a fraction of a second per swing.

What at first appears to be a faster swing, in other words, may simply be a *shorter* swing. Similarly, the pro who struggles to keep his tour card because his transition from backswing to forward swing is riddled with loops or hitches— think Nick Price, circa 1985—can shed up to four frames of unsightly video simply by eliminating those moves. Again, the pro isn't just swinging faster; he's swinging *more efficiently.*

The second explanation for faster swings comes from the guy on TV doing one-arm push-ups with his toes planted on a wobbly exercise ball. "The modern golfer," he says between sets, "is an *athlete.* He's bigger, stronger, faster and more flexible than the pros of twenty years ago." Tiger Woods launched the trend by packing thirty pounds of golf-specific muscle onto his willowy 6-foot frame, and now any tour player who aspires to be No. 50, much less No. 1, spends a couple of hours a day stretching, balancing, lifting, rowing and running.

"Athletes," our trainer friend continues, "swing *athletically*. Their Holy Grail is clubhead speed, and they've figured out that the power guys, like Dustin Johnson or Bubba Watson, swing fast and hard."

Both explanations strike me as valid. When I time a pro who has made a significant swing change, his elapsed time is either the same or shorter than it was before the overhaul; it's never longer. The fitness paradigm also rings true. In the rare instance where I clock a prime-of-career pro swinging slower than normal, it's invariably late in the golf season, when fatigue and injury have taken their toll. The other swing-speed regulator is Old Man Time. Some tour players pick up a frame on the downswing in their forties, when their bodies begin to cry, "*No Mas!*"*

But while these two theories satisfy up to a point, I suspect a third mover behind the trend toward faster swings: *Tour Tempo,* the book.

————

Let's be clear. I'm not claiming that tour players have *better* tempo today than they had in the spring of 2004, when the book came out. Tour tempo is exactly what it was when Bobby Jones was winning grand-slam events: a consistent 3-to-1 time ratio of backswing to forward swing.

But in the decades before *Tour Tempo,* a certain paradigm ruled golf. I call it "the cult of low-and-slow" after the prevalent theory that the club should be taken back very deliberately with the clubhead hugging the ground—a well-intentioned piece of advice that had millions of amateurs swinging as if they had arthritis on the backswing and St. Vitus's Dance into the ball.

I'm sure my assault on low-and-slow hurt the feelings of a great many teaching pros. I know it didn't make me popular with the many fans and disciples of the great Bobby Jones, whose famous quote—"Nobody ever swung a golf club too slowly"—was picked apart by my co-author in the book's introduction.

The tour pros themselves believed in low-and-slow. Asked to define good tempo, they used words like "unhurried," "smooth," and "oily." When advising duffers in pro-ams, they said, "You're jumpin' at the ball," or "Swing easy," or "You tryin' to hit it 300 yards with your backswing?" Their own bad shots they invariably blamed on "getting quick under pressure." Their winning shots

*Vijay Singh is a good example. He has picked up two frames as he approaches fifty, going from 24/8 to 24/10. That has made him more erratic from tee to green.

found the mark "because I didn't get ahead of myself" or "because I remembered to take a deep breath and slow down" or—my favorite—"because I pretended I only had to hit it halfway to the hole."

It's not that the pros were trying to mislead us. They *did* hit most of their tee shots at about 80-percent of full effort. Too-quick transitions from back-swing to forward swing *did* cause their weak long-iron shots and fatted wedges. And Bobby Jones truly *believed* he was swinging slowly, despite the fact that his 27/9 action was identical to that of Tiger Woods, *circa* 1997.

We were all misled by our perceptions. The pros, who had been swinging full-bore since they were kids, didn't realize that their "slow" was way, way faster than the mid-handicapper's "fast." The swing gurus, obsessed as they were with drawing lines on TV screens, didn't recognize that their frame-by-frame analysis de-emphasized the dynamic nature of the golf swing. And those of us watching from behind the ropes or on TV simply believed our lying eyes. A few wise men knew that the pros' perfect tempos made their golf swings look slower than they really were—but those wise men weren't in charge of the paradigm.

Tour Tempo put an end to the low-and-slow paradigm.

Chapter 15

Tiger Watch

"In my opinion, Tiger ruined the greatest swing and the greatest physique in golf history."

—Brandel Chamblee

There's one question that I'm asked over and over: How did Tiger Woods's tempo get so screwed up? Tiger is very secretive, so we may never know. It's clear that his swing sped up significantly in 2004, when he started working with Hank Haney. And when I say sped up, I mean Tiger went from a dependable 24/8 to a denominator-7 or denominator-6 swing, taking anywhere from 17 to 22 frames on the backswing. His head began to bob excessively, which is something a duffer does. That can cause all sorts of mis-hits.

You can't blame the faster swing for Tiger's problems; lesser pros speed up without losing their mechanics. Possibly the answer lies in his physical problems—the knee surgeries, the ankle strains, the toll that decades of high-torque rotation have taken on his hips, back and neck. All I know is, Tiger used to be one of the best ever at keeping his spine angle on the downswing. By the spring of 2011, he was one of the worst on tour.

Tempo is no longer a mysterious entity that can't be measured or adjusted, so I continue to clock Tiger's swings, looking for signs that he's abandoned his never-ending process and rediscovered his incomparable feel. Here, edited for brevity, are my 2011 progress reports on Woods, from his first tournament in January through the PGA Championship in August:

Farmers Insurance Open, San Diego, Calif., January 27–30

(TIGER WOODS: 69-69-74-75—287; Finish: T44. Prize money: $18,096. Driving Accuracy: T50. Driving Distance: 296.0 (40th). Putts Per GIR: 1.813 (63rd). Greens in Reg: 66.7% (T26). Sand Saves: 54.5% (25th).

Shot	Tempo	Outcome	Comment
Drive on No. 1, R1	26/7	Missed fwy	Sluggish swingaway, at least 2 frames slow to 2nd checkpoint
35′ birdie putt on No. 6, R1	18/8	Made	Good stroke
10′ putt for great par save on 8, R1	20/7	Made	It's his driver tempo, but putt dropped
Drive on par-5 9th, R1	25/7	Rt rough	4 frames too slow to 2nd checkpoint; w/out those 4 frames he's a perfect 21/7
10′ birdie putt on 9th, R1	16/7	Misses right	Forward stroke rushed a frame
5′ putt on 15th, R2	16/6	Miss	More a stab than a stroke
38-foot eagle putt on 18, R2	16/8	Barely misses	Must be practicing his tempo

ANALYSIS: A Jekyll & Hyde performance by Tiger—two sharp rounds followed by an awful weekend. His backswing times are slower, which would be fine if he could get back his old 8-frame forward swing. Instead he's flirting with a low-and-slow takeaway—sort of like pairing a coat and tie with bathing trunks. I give him a solid B for his short game, though. Lots of 16s for the tempo numerator. Tiger's take: "It feels better. It's an evolution."

Omega Dubai Desert Classic, United Arab Emirates, Feb. 10–13

(TIGER WOODS: 71-66-72-75—284; Finish: T20; Driving Accuracy: 44.6% (59th); Driving Distance: 296.6 (7th); Greens in Reg: 65.3% (38th); Putts Per GIR: 1.578 (2nd); Putts Per Round: 27.8 (8th); Sand Saves: 33.3%.)

Shot	Tempo	Outcome	Comment
First tee shot of tourney, 3-wood	23/7	Middle of fairway	Nice
Iron approach, R1	22/7	5 feet	Double Nice!
5' putt for birdie, H1	16/7	Made	Locked in on 7?
Approach shot R1 GC	20/7	Off back of green	Nothing wrong w/tempo; wrong club?
Downhill chip, R1 GC	16/9	Announcer: "He flubbed it."	Classic decel!
4' for par, R1	16/7	Made	Consistent 7 frames on putts
Drive R2 GC	23/6	Lands in adjacent fairway	4-to-1! Danger, Will Robinson! Danger!
5' putt R1	17/7	Made	Takeaway 3 frames too slow
Drive on par-5 H18 R1	22/7	Fairway	Missing parallel position by 2 frames (See analysis)
H18 approach, R1	21/8	Dunked in pond	Brisk backswing, lazy forward swing.

Shot	Tempo	Outcome	Comment
Hole 12 approach, R2	21/7	To 3'	Textbook
H4 full swing, R2	24/6	4:1 crazy, but good shot	Partner Lee Westwood also swinging 24/6! Coincidence?
Iron approach, 3-quarter swing	22/7	To 2'	Anncr: "He's playing very well today."
Full swing, R2	22/6	To 2nd cut back of green	Needs to smother that 6 with a pillow
H12 Drive, R4	24/6	Rt fairway bunker	Funny little 1-frame delay at the top
8' par putt on 14, R4	18/7	Missed, pushed rt	4 frames slow on takeaway

ANALYSIS: Tiger is close to locking in a 7-frame downswing. Or he looks to be, anyway, until he's paired with a faster-swinging player like Lee Westwood or until the wind starts to blow, as it did on the weekend. (Gusty winds disrupt even the best players' tempos.) More worrisome, he's taking 11 or 12 frames to get the shaft parallel to the ground on his takeaway, which is a couple of frames too slow. (See the "5-10-15 Concept," Chapter 10.) He's also dithering at the top. It's just a one- or two-frame delay, but the old Tiger did not dither; his hands reversed their path with no delays at the top.

WGC-Accenture Match Play Championship, Tucson, Ariz., Feb. 23–27

(TIGER WOODS: Loses first-day match to Thomas Bjorn in 19 holes for T-33 finish and $45,000. No official stats released due to match play format. Tiger falls to No. 5 in World Ranking, his lowest position since rookie season.)

Shot	Tempo	Outcome	Comment
1st tee driver, M1 vs. Thomas Bjorn	22/7	Fwy	Great swing
No. 1 approach	20/7	Airmailed it; flew the green	Good motion

Shot	Tempo	Outcome	Comment
No. 1, 14' for par	15/8	Missed short, Bjorn wins hole	Close to old optimum of 16/8
No. 2, greenside bunker on par 5	21/8	To 8'	Full-swing tempo from bunker
8' putt for birdie	14/6	Made, squares match	Good result, but hurried stroke
H3 Iron shot, 208-yd par-3	20/7	In water, wide right and short	Nothing wrong with tempo, but got under ball
Chip on 6	15/8	To 6"—Bjorn bogey, T wins hole	Sweet
No. 7, iron off desert	23/7	To 4'	Great shot
4' putt on 7 to square match	11/6	Made	11-frame backswing very fast
No. 10, 178-yd approach	20/7	To 7'. Bjorn concedes 2nd straight hole, match square	Consistent 7s on downswing; good sign
Par-5 11th, 2nd from fairway, 290 to hole	20/6	Pushed right onto cart path, but wins hole with birdie, goes 1-up	6-frame downswing spells trouble
No. 12, pitch from rough	16/8	To 10'	Tour Tempo
Par-5 13th, 2nd shot	19/7	In front of green. Bjorn birdie squares match	Announcer: "This is going right …"
Pitch for eagle on 15	18/9	To 6'	Great tempo
No. 17 3-wood tee shot	22/7	Fwy	Best-looking swing of day; no dithering
17th approach, 172 yds	22/7	Pin-high, 9'	Another good-looking swing, on plane

Shot	Tempo	Outcome	Comment
9' birdie try on 17	17/7	Missed, Bjorn stays 1-up	Missed opportunity
No. 18 approach	21/7	To 7'	Clutch
7' birdie putt on 18 to extend match	14/7	Made	Fist-pump; Tiger of old? On to sudden-death
19th hole of Bjorn match, 3-wood tee shot	22/7	Disaster, into cacti in desert right	Not a bad swing, but goose cooked. Takes 2 swipes to escape desert
19th hole, 4th shot approach	21/7	10'	Tour Tempo, but too late
10' bogey putt	17/8	To 1'	Bjorn wins match, 1-up, 19 holes. Tiger goes home.

ANALYSIS: Announcer Kelly Tilgman's take on Tiger—"moments of brilliance and struggle"—is accurate. Lots of superb swings at or close to 21/7 and plenty of chips and putts at the desired 2-to-1, but the consistency is still lacking. Tiger looked like the Tiger of old on 18, which he had to birdie to extend the match. But he couldn't find the fairway with a 3-wood on the playoff hole. And that's the Tiger of late.

WGC-Cadillac Championship, Doral, Fla., March 10–13

(TIGER WOODS: 70-74-70-66—280. Finish: T10. Prize money: $129,000. Driving distance: 299.9 yds. Driving accuracy: 46.4%. Greens in reg: 72.4% (T4). Putts per round: 29.0 (T55). Great final round with only 25 putts boosts Woods to $129,000 paycheck and first top-10 finish of 2011.)

Shot	Tempo	Outcome	Comment
R1 3-wd tee shot on par-5 10th	20/7	Fwy	Good start
R1 10th green 8' birdie putt	17/6	Miss	Betrayed by short game

Shot	Tempo	Outcome	Comment
R1 par-4 11th, 402 yds, iron off tee	20/8	Middle fwy, frnt of palms & bunker	Instead of swinging fwd, it's like his dipping starts club back to ball
R1 H11 approach, ¾-swing	21/7	Flies green into bunker	Can't fault tempo
R1 11th bunker shot	20/8	To 13′	Blah
Par-5 12th, R1, Driver	21/6	Left into trees	Announcer: "Tiger's pretty disgusted with that swing."
R1 H12 2nd shot out of rough	22/6	Lofted over trees into fwy	Nice recovery
Iron off tee on par-3 13th, R1	19/7	lft greenside bnkr	Set up for cut, it didn't cut
R1 14th approach, 173 yds	22/7	To 10′	Good shot, but 12 frames to parallel
10′ birdie putt, R1 H14	16/6	Miss	Anncr 1: "Didn't take that back very far"; Anncr 2: "Kind of short and quick."
No. 15 Driver on short par 4, R1, cutting across dogleg	19/7	fwy in front of traps	Faster bckswng
17th green, R1 12′ for bird	15/7	Miss	Frustrated
189-yd approach on par 5 1st, R1	21/7	To 8′ for eagle chance	Sweet
8′ eagle putt, H1 R1	16/7	Miss	Anncr: "Tiger's trying to get the right release with the putter."

Shot	Tempo	Outcome	Comment
No. 2, R1, 146-yd approach	24/8	To 25′	Tiger's old tempo, when he played his best
168-yd approach, No. 3, R1	22/7	To 9′	Tiger starting to click
R1 H3 9′ birdie putt	17/7	Made for birdie	Arm pump
Tee shot, par 3 4th, R1	21/6	Iron into lft rough	Anncr: "Moving around like his left leg is hurting."
Approach on par-4 5th, R1	20/6	To 6′	Really sticking his irons
145-yd approach from fwy No. 6, R2	20/7	To 12′	Tempo definitely better w irons
115 yd. 3rd on 8th, R2	22/7	To 5′	Really locking in on 7 frame downswing
5′ birdie putt, H8 R2	14/7	Miss	Wasn't his tempo; misread?
3-wd tee shot, par-5 10th, R2	23/7	Pushed way right	Looks like he's setting up to ball with shoulders open
3rd from fwy bunker, No. 10 R2	21/7	To 24′	Excellent
3-wood tee shot on 14, R2	21/7	Fat, hit 6″ behind ball; flies only 188 yds	Anncr: "My wife says I could have outdriven Tiger on that hole." [Really odd. Actually 1 of his better swings.]
5′ putt on No. 17, R2	16/7	Miss	Putter wandering all over

ANALYSIS: *Tiger continues with his inconsistent tempos and struggles with his mechanics. He hit one of the worst drives of his career—a 3-wood duck hook that flew 188 yards to the left. Ouch! But he still finished in a tie for tenth. Go figure.*

Arnold Palmer Invitational, Orlando, Fla., March 24–27

(TIGER WOODS: 73-68-74-72—287. Finish: T24. Prize money: $48,600. Driving distance: 272.9 (63rd). Driving accuracy: 51.8 (71st). Greens in regulation: 63.9% (T34). Putts per Round: 29.0 (24th). Putts per GIR: 1.804 (T30). Bogeys: 10. Double bogeys: 2.

Shot	Tempo	Outcome	Comment
8th, R1 20' putt	16/8	Made	Great stroke
R1 H11 iron approach	21/7	To 12'	Tour Tempo
R1 H12 pitch	18/9	Hit flagstick	Amazing correlation between perfect tempo and flagstick hits
R3 12th hole approach over water from fwy bunker	24/7	Splash!	24/7, but 14 frames to get clubshaft parallel; 20 yds short
R4 10th, ¾ wedge approach	23/9	To 12'	'tweener tempo
R4 13th approach	21/6	To 22'	1 frame off TT
R4, No. 14 iron on par 3	21/7	Lft greensd bkr	Can't blame tempo
R4 H14 6' par putt	15/7	Missed	Tiger doesn't look happy

ANALYSIS: Can't blame him for not looking happy. Mediocre numbers by his standards. But hey, he's gonna do better in a couple of weeks at the Masters.

The Masters, Augusta, Ga., April 7–10

(TIGER WOODS: 71-66-74-67—278. Finish: T4. Prize money: $330,667. Avg. driving distance: 287.75 yds. Fairways hit: 37 of 56 (66.07%). Greens in reg: 53 of 72 (73.61%). Sand saves: 2 of 3. Putts per round: 30.0. Eagles: 1. Birdies: 19. Bogeys: 11. Final-round charge falters on back nine, but Woods shows flashes of his best game and pockets $330,667 for his week's work. Surly

at the end, Woods withholds the fact that he re-injured his left knee hitting off the pine straw on No. 17.)

Shot	Tempo	Outcome	Comment
Par-3 16th, R1	21/7	To 15'	Tour Tempo
R1 H17, iron from lft rough	21/7	Over the green	21/7 is perfect for Tiger 3.0. Distance control will follow consistency
No. 18 drive, R1	21/6	Stops short of left fwy bunker	Downswing just a frame fast
182-yd 8-iron approach, uphill, R1 H18	21/7	To 6'	Missed putt spoils a string of great swings
R2, par-5 8th Driver	21/7	289 yards uphill in fwy	Perfect; tending great
281-yd scnd shot, uphill	21/7	Just off green, good shot, leads to birdie	Tiger dialing in that 21/7, very encouraging
Par-3 6th tee shot, R4	21/7	To 5'	1 problem w his 21/7s; gets to 20, lowers body & club (1 frame), then 7 down
5' birdie putt H6 R4	14/7	Made	Perfection
No. 8 R4 fwy wood 2nd shot uphill	22/6	Bounces off right bank and rolls up green to 8' for eagle try	Brilliant. Vintage Tiger
8' eagle putt, No. 8, R4	17/8, no unnecessary frame pauses	Made for eagle! Tiger arm pump is a haymaker swing	5-under on front side, 10-under for tournament, making historic charge. Shares lead with McIlroy & Schwarzel when Rory bogeys 5

Shot	Tempo	Outcome	Comment
No. 12 4' par putt R4	18/7	Power lip-out, l to r	Too-slow back-swing. Bogey blunts his charge, trails McIlroy by 2
Par-5 15th, R4, 2nd shot	20/6	Covers flag, stops 4' from hole	Blogger: "Tiger may well have just played the defining shot of this year's tournament."
H15 R4 3' for eagle	18/4	Jab miss, lips out right; he'll settle for birdie	Blogger: "That was spectacularly inept … He looks sick."
72nd hole fwy wood tee shot, Tiger yells "Bite! Bite!"	21/7	Stops just off cor-ner left fwy bunker, great position	Great swing under pressure
H18 R4 approach	19/6	Frnt of green right, not close	2-putt par makes Tiger leader in clubhouse at 10-under, but Schwarzel birdies in to win at 14-under. Tiger curt in interviews.

ANALYSIS: The most encouraging week for Woods since he hit that hydrant. His full swing seems to be settling at 21/7 (classic Tour Tempo), and he had streaks of ball-striking reminiscent of his best years. He made a bunch of birdie putts, too, many of them with a denominator-7 stroke. On the other hand, Tiger's 21/7 has a noticeable flaw: that puzzling body-drop during transition that consumes one or two frames. (Under Butch Harmon, Tiger maintained his posture through impact and the club changed directions at the top with no dithering.) Tiger also missed some pressure putts with a stroke that could only be described as yippy. Still, I'd give him a B or a B-plus.

THE PLAYERS Championship, Ponte Vedra Beach, Fla., May 12–15

(TIGER WOODS: Withdraws in first round due to knee injury after scoring 42 for nine holes. It's the same knee, his left, that was surgically repaired in 2008. Tiger says he re-injured it in the final round of the Masters.)

Shot	Tempo	Outcome	Comment
R1 H1 iron approach	20/6	Into lft rough, hurt knee on shot	Too fast down
R1 pitch on 4th	20/9	First of 2 balls in water on way to triple-bogey 7	Just like before: way too slow on early bckswng

ANALYSIS: Biomechanics expert Bob Prichard blames Tiger's knee problems on an incorrect spine angle caused by his new swing. "His swing is measurably worse in every way," Prichard told the New York Times, "and is putting extra strain on his left knee. More than ever, he is pushing his hip toward the target, outside his left foot, and the stress is going into his left knee, actually pushing the femur down on to the tibial plate." Whatever the cause, Tiger's injury sidelines him just when he seemed to be regaining his tempo. And nobody knows when he'll return.)

WGC-Bridgestone Invitational, Akron, Ohio, August 4–7

(TIGER WOODS: 68-71-72-70—281. Finish: T37. Prize money: $58,500. Driving distance: 316 yds (9th). Driving accuracy: 39.3% (76th in 76-man field). Greens in regulation: 65.3% (T26). Putts per GIR: 1.745 (T26). Putts per round: 29.3 (T43).

Shot	Tempo	Outcome	Comment
R1 H1 fwy wood tee shot	24/6	Rt. fwy bunker	Way off at 4/1, 1 frame dither at the top
R1 H1 iron approach	22/7	On green, 30'	Much better
No. 2 tee driver, R1	24/6	Rt. fwy bunker	1 frame delay at top as he lowers body and club

Shot	Tempo	Outcome	Comment
R1 H2 30' putt	16/8	To 1 inch	Vintage Tiger
R1 3rd tee fwy wood	22/7	Rt. side fwy	Close to ideal
No. 3, R1 147-yd 9-iron approach	23/6	Flew over green	Still 12 frames to parallel, chckpt. 2
R1 H3, chip from 18'	20/8	14' short	Faldo: "He hit that a little fat." [slow backswing]
R1 4th tee driver	23/7	Left sd fwy, 320 yds	Solid
R1 H4 123-yd approach	23/8	To 10'	Close to his old 24/8
R1 H4 12' for birdie	19/7	Miss	3 or 4 frame freeze during transition
5th hole 6-iron, R1	23/7	To 9'	Best shots are denominator-7s
R1 8th Driver	23/7	Rough	Didn't fade, almost hit camera crew
R1 H8 approach, 156 yds	23/6	Rt. greensd bunker	4-to-1; backswing too slow or fwd swing too fast
R1 H8 bunker shot	21/10	To 8'	Great example of slo-mo sand tempo
R1 H8 8' for par	16/8	Made	Perfect Tiger tempo
R1 H9 177 yd trouble shot	21/7	Hooked into rough left of green	Perfect tempo, just overcooked the hook
R3 H15 par-3, 206-yd 6-iron	21/8	To 5'	Even par at time, but didn't hit a fwy 'til 11th hole. Tiger says problem is he's driving it "straighter than before." (!!!!)

Shot	Tempo	Outcome	Comment
R3 H16 par-5, 69-yd pitch	21/8	Flies green into back bunker, long by 8-10 yds	Bubba Watson: "You've got to think he's just rusty."
R3 H16, bunker shot	23/8	To 8'	Full-swing tempo
R3 17th fwy, 164-yd approach	21/7	Middle of green	Tour Tempo
R3 No. 18, 30' birdie putt	19/8	To 3'	3 frame pause at top; stroke not reflexive
R3 18th, 3' putt for par and 71	17/8	Misses hole completely on left, goes 3' by	2 frame pause at top

ANALYSIS: *Returning from a three-month injury layoff as the world's 28th-ranked golfer—and having recently fired his longtime caddie, Steve Williams—Tiger impresses the analysts by shooting two-under in the first round. "The most impressive thing was the tempo, the rhythm of the golf swing," says Golf Channel's Nick Faldo, crediting Tiger's "funny little boat shoes" (a pair of Nike softspikes) for keeping him "softer and quieter .... Any time he forces a shot he loses a massive amount of level." SI's Gary Van Sickle agrees, writing, "His swing looks better, more balanced. He isn't dropping his head like he was last year." The subsequent rounds are not as encouraging, with Woods missing most fairways and a lot of greens. Tiger's explanation is that he is hitting it so good that he doesn't know his distances, causing him to misclub. He says, "I'm hitting the ball numbers I've never hit before." Tiger's tempo stats paint a less rosy picture. He's consistently slow to the first checkpoint on the full swing, and his putting suffers from a two-to-three frame pause at the top before the forward stroke.*

The PGA Championship, Atlanta, Ga., August 11–14

(TIGER WOODS: 77-73—150; Finish: T116, Missed Cut. Measured drive average: 312 yds. Fairways hit: 12 of 28, 42.9%. Greens in Regulation: 20 of 36, 55.6%. Sand saves: 4 of 11, 36.4%. Putts per round: 28.5. Birdies: 8. Bogeys: 8. Double-bogeys: 5.)

Shot	Tempo	Outcome	Comment
10th hole (T's first), R1, approach from fwy bunker	25/8	To 20'	Hopeful sign: no frames wasted on pulldown frm top
3rd shot, par-5 12th, R1	18/9	To 2' for tap-in birdie	Perfect short-game tempo
No. 14 approach, R1	22/8	To 3', another bird	Again, no pull down; but denominator-8? Going back to Harmon swing?
Par-3 15th, 253 yds over water, R1	21/7	Splash, short by a yard or so. Double-bogey	1-frame pulldown
H18, R1 long approach frm fwy bunker over water	22/8	Lft greenside bunker	2-frame pulldown; makes turn +2 after reaching 3-under
No. 6 approach frm fwy bunker, R1	21/8	Splash, another double, +6	Sure hitting out of a lot of twy bunkers
No. 9, R1, TW's finishing hole, frm fwy bunker	21/10	To 15'	Wrong tempo, right shot
2nd Round, 1st tee fwy wood	24/7	rt fwy bunker	12 frames back to 2nd checkpt., should be 10
H1 R2 fwy bunker shot	21/7	greenside bunker	1-frame pulldown
2nd hole escape shot from hardpan rt of cart path, R2	22/7	Back of green	No wasted frames at top
Par-3 4th 183-yd 7-iron, R2	21/7	45' pin-high left	Tour Tempo
Par-5 5th driver, R2	22/7	Rt. fwy bunker	Anncr: "He has been in some bunkers."

Shot	Tempo	Outcome	Comment
H5 R2 3rd to green	20/8	Flies green, plugs in bunker on downslope	D. Feherty: "He's not going to be cheerful when he sees that."
25' for par, H5 R2	18/8	To 3"	Lagging many of his putts this week
6th tee fwy wood, R2	23/7	Middle fwy (!!!)	12 frames to ckpt. 2
H7 birdie try, R2	17/7 w/ 2-frame pause at top	Halfway to the hole	Anncr: "Worst putt I ever saw Tiger hit … Did he hit his foot? He hit it fat!"
H7 6' par putt	19/7	Miss	Nowhere near Tour Tempo
No. 8 8-iron approach R2	25/7	To 12'	25?
12' birdie putt, H8 R2	18/7	Made	3-frame pause at top
H9 R2 Driver	22/7	Middle fwy	Getting close
H9 121-yd approach	21/8	To 6'	1 of best swings, hit all chckpts; Anncr: "That was a perfect swing, wasn't it?"
No. 10 tee fwy wood	25/8	fwy	Anncr: "Four in a row that have been really good."
H10 R2 30' birdie putt	16/8	To 2'	1 of his best putts
Fwy bunker approach, H11 R2	22/8	Bunker to bunker	Anncr: "Tiger's caddie is raking more bunkers in 2 days than Steve Williams did in 13 years."

Shot	Tempo	Outcome	Comment
H11 R2 difficult bunker shot frm behind green	19/3/6 [3-frame pause at top, possibly to maintain balance]	Across green into water	Almost impossible stance; 1 foot in bunker, 1 foot out
12th tee Driver, R1	24/6	Huge hook into trees	4/1 swing, Tiger doesn't even react to horrible shot
Fwy wood 3rd shot after punching out frm trees H12, R2	23/7	Hideous	Anncr: "Huge left into the trees, hit a tree & kicked left, a smother hook"
4th shot, off pine needles H12 R2	21/7	To 20 yds in front of green	Actually 1 of his better swings
5th shot pitch H12 R2	17/9	To 6'	Good shot
H12 R2, 6' for bogey	15/7	Miss, makes 2nd straight double	Possibly worst 2 hole stretch I've ever seen from T
No. 13, R2 2nd shot from fwy bunker	24/8	To 2' for easy birdie	Wonderful shot, perfect tempo
17 tee, R2	23/7	Over green into bunker	More sand!
Long fwy bunker approach over water, H18 R2	23/7	Splash left, not close	Silly shot, but he's past caring
From drop area, H18 R2	20/8	To 3'	One of his better swings
3' putt H18 R2	18/8	Made for bogey	Tiger's weekend plans not known

ANALYSIS: *Tiger was in 22 bunkers in two days, more than ten per round. He went bunker-to-bunker seven times. He had five double-bogeys. He hit hooks and slices. He also hit a number of tour pro-quality shots—but not enough to make a difference. By Tiger standards, he was terrible. He started great, getting to three-under on Thursday morning; but that, he said after the round, was when he was focused on swing mechanics. "Every shot I hit up to that point were all mechanical thoughts, I put the club in a certain position. And I said, 'You know what, I'm feeling good, let's just let it go.' And it cost me the whole round." He said, in other words, that he has lost his ability to play by feel. Which, if you're Tiger Woods, is an absolute catastrophe. Tiger added, "I'm really angry right now."*

Which was understandable because the great man was simply lost. Asked on Friday afternoon what adjustments he was going to have to make to fix his game, Woods said, "It's going to be a lot. It's a laundry list."

Tiger, can we talk? Let's rethink this! It's not a laundry list. It's not a 20-point checklist. It's not any kind of list. What you need is a paradigm shift. You need to think less and feel more. Most of all, you need to restore your confidence, and the best way to do that is to restore your once-great tempo.

Chapter 16

Case Studies

CASE STUDY 143-06
Name: Padraig Harrington
Occupation: PGA Tour professional   **Age:** 40
Driving Average (2005): 293.9 yards (54th)
Driving Accuracy (2005): 54.61% (189th)
Scoring Average (2005): 70.84 (72nd)
Self-Evaluation: (2006) "I'm a much better player than I was last year, and I had two wins last year. But I haven't come close this year, barring the U.S. Open at Winged Foot. And I was very disappointed there. You know, three pars to win the Open. I certainly ruined that one. It's just a strange game. I'm kind of putting it down to I've changed a few things in my game. I'm putting it down to transition more than anything else. But I feel really good about my game, I've never felt as confident or relaxed going into tournaments." [Laughs] "Maybe I need to go back to a fearful panic before a tournament."
Trainer: John Novosel Jr.
Training Site: Southern Hills C.C., Tulsa, Okla.

Diagnosis: Padraig began working with our SpeedBall training aid in 2006, the year he topped the European Tour money list for the first time. Already a three-time Ryder Cupper and a two-time winner on the PGA Tour, he was runner-up in the Players Championship in 2003 and 2004, T5 at the 2002 Masters, and fifth in the 2002 and 2006 U.S. Opens. Padraig's tempo for most of that period was 25/8, so he needed no correction there. His short game was extraordinary, one of the best ever tested by the Titleist Performance Institute. Paddy thought if he could gain ten or so yards with his driver, he'd be able to reach more par-5s in two and have more wedge approaches to the par-4s.

Training Report: Padraig wanted to meet on a Tuesday morning at Tulsa's Southern Hills Country Club. Not *any* Tuesday morning, however, but the week of the 2007 PGA Championship. It was a hot, muggy morning, but I found him at the back end of the driving range. We started to talk about what it takes to create speed and power. He asked me what I was working on and if I would look at a couple of things he was doing. Anyway, he said, "Why don't you come and walk a few holes with me, we'll keep talking." So I walked with him for a few holes, answering his questions about tempo and the SpeedBall drills. He finally said, "You know, it's hard to talk out here. Why don't you have dinner with us?"

So I met Padraig and his wife Caroline that night at a Japanese steak house. We were joined by the mental coach/author Bob Rotella; Padraig's caddie, Ronan; Padraig's Ryder Cup teammate, Paul McGinley, and a few wives were sprinkled in. As we were being seated, one of the wives said, "Padraig, can I sit by you?" He grinned and said, "Sure, if you want to talk about clubhead speed." Laughing and rolling her eyes, she sat down with the other wives, leaving me the chair between Padraig and Rotella. What followed was a high-spirited, witty, meandering, and stimulating dinner. A *business* dinner.

Afterwards, we drove back to the Harrington's rental house. Padraig and I were clearing the living room of furniture when Caroline walked by. "What are you doing?" she asked. He explained, "We need room to swing." A typical golfer/wife exchange! The only difference was this golfer was trying to win his second major against a field that included Tiger Woods at the top of his game.

I think of it as *Amazing moment #44.* Padraig had worked on his game in the Tulsa heat for six or seven hours, and now it was close to 9:30—but the guy was non-stop! He set up the SpeedBall impact target, and I played the 21/7 Tour Tempo tones on my iPod. Padraig then started thumping the target with his SpeedBall club, swinging to the tones. Swing after swing, the velcro-faced clubhead met the target with a satisfying thwack and a perfectly balanced follow-through.

Follow-Up: Eleven months later, Harrington won the 2008 Open Championship at Royal Birkdale. Three weeks after that, he won his *third* major, the PGA Championship at Oakland Hills CC, and climbed to No. 3 in the World Ranking. Harrington was the first Irish winner of the PGA and the first European winner of the PGA since Tommy Armour in 1930. Padraig also picked up a few yards with his driver, averaging 296.3 and ranking 32nd in 2008. His most recent wins are the 2009 Irish PGA Championship and the 2010 Iskandar Johor Open (Asian Tour).

A 25/8 when we first timed him, he's now a wicked-fast 19/6. That's pretty damn fast for a 40-year-old body, but Padraig is as diligent in the gym as he is on the range. At mid-season, 2011, his PGA Tour driving distance average was 293.8 yards, which ranked 49th.

CASE STUDY 102-08

Name: Phil Mickelson

Occupation: PGA Tour professional   **Age:** 40

Average Driving Distance (2008): 295.7 yards (35th)

Driving Accuracy (2008): 55.27% (181st)

Scoring Average (2008): 69.17 (2nd)

Self-Evaluation: [August, 2008] "I have looked back on this last year, and the area that I've been most deficient in is putting. So I've tried to target that." On leaving longtime swing coach Rick Smith for Butch Harmon: "I think sometimes you just need to hear something from a little different point of view. But I've been very pleased with the swing changes that we have made. I notice when I see my swing on TV, how much shorter and more compact it looks, and easier to repeat. And it feels that way, as well."

Trainer: John Novosel Jr.

Diagnosis: Phil's problems went a lot deeper than the flat stick. Dad had a substantial folder of Mickelson videos, particularly shots around the green.

Mickelson's short game was so great and so creative that it was fun just to watch him pinch the ball or lob it, spin it or let it roll out. Dad timed Phil chipping in for a birdie at the 2008 PGA Championship, and Phil's tempo fraction was 18/9—the perfect 2-to-1 short-game tempo. But Dad also had recent videos of Lefty hitting uncharacteristically poor greenside shots in majors—a chunked chip; a bladed chip that raced clear across the green; a flop shot *into* a bunker. Phil's short-game tempo was unpredictable. He'd stroke one putt at 13/7 and then stroke another at 17/8. Then he'd hit a pitch shot at 18/9.

Thinking *This is a job for Tour Tempo!*, I sent Phil a Micro Player and waited to hear back. Imagine my surprise when Phil called to say that Tour Tempo was helping a lot with his full swing, but not so much around the greens.

Huh? That made no sense at all.

And just so you know, I'd heard those rumors that Phil wasn't the nicest guy in the world. But he was. He was extremely gracious and very polite. And *cerebral*. I've met some brainy golfers, but Mickelson could give most of them ten IQ points a side.

After watching Phil putt, chip, pitch and hit bunker shots, I realized that he didn't actually have a short-game tempo. He had short-game *tempos*—a tempo for every variety of turfgrass, for every kind of greenside lie, for every degree of risk and reward. Phil was a Mozart of golf, and I felt like some latter-day Solieri telling him that there was only one short-game tempo.

Thanks to Phil, I've kind of softened my stance on that point. Not every shot has to have the same frame count. Your chipping tempo doesn't have to be identical to your lob-swing tempo. (Just make sure you're 2-to-1.) But Phil—oh man, he was doing all kinds of crazy stuff. He's mastered so many finesse shots—like that backwards-over-his-head bunker shot that blows people's minds—that having the same frame count on every greenside swing isn't necessarily part of his equation any more.

What could I say? Rules are made to be broken. Besides, it was no small thing that tempo training was helping Phil keep his full swing in tune.

Follow-Up: Phil won three PGA Tour events in 2009 and then won the 2010 Masters with a final-round 67. That final round included one of the most memorable shots in golf history—a 6-iron off pine needles through a narrow gap between trees and over Rae's creek onto the thirteenth green for birdie. (His tempo on that shot was 21/8.) Phil's putting, it has to be said, has remained inconsistent.

Here's the point I make to the average golfer: "You're not Phil. You need a dependable chip shot, a dependable flop shot, a dependable bunker shot … and one tempo for all three, because the average golfer is never going to have the time or the talent to master five variations of the chip and four variations of the flop."

CASE STUDY 73-07

Name: Garrett Willis

Occupation: PGA Tour professional   **Age:** 37

Average Driving Distance (2006): 283.6 (147th)

Driving Accuracy (2006): 68.63% (32nd)

Putts Per Round (2006): 28.85 (40th)

Self-Evaluation (2011): "If I can hit the driver, control the golf ball and make some putts, I'm going to finish pretty decent. … A lot of times my problem is I get too aggressive on the golf course, and that's based on my putting. If I felt like I could make some 15-footers, I wouldn't feel like I have to aim at so many pins and short-side myself. Because the frustration builds when you short-side yourself. You chip up to five feet, and it just sort of snowballs."

Trainer: John Novosel Jr.

Training Site: Tampa, Fla.

Diagnosis: Garrett has six victories as a pro, but his claim to fame is winning his very first start as a member of the PGA Tour, the 2001 Tucson Open. He came to us through Arnie Cunningham, who contacted me at the 2009 PGA Merchandise Show. "Garrett's like every other tour pro, looking for more distance," Arnie explained, "and after my experience with Tour Tempo, I think it would be a good idea if you guys could train together." So I flew down to Florida to work with Garrett. We hit it off, and we started doing Tour Tempo and the SpeedBall together. Garrett did see some increase in clubhead speed from using the SpeedBall, and he really liked using the Micro Player before a round. For him, the tempo tones are a focus mechanism. They help quiet his mind and get him ready for a round. They establish his swing rhythm.

It goes back to my dad's theory of why Tour Tempo works. No matter how technical you get with your swing, doing the tones drowns out the prescriptions and proscriptions, the hopes and fears, the pointless distractions. The effect is almost hypnotic. Garrett's goal for the year was to get his PGA Tour card back. (He achieved that goal, with over $260,000 in winnings and a 12th-place finish on the Nationwide money list.)

Follow-Up: "When I putt well, I play well," Garrett says. In 2010, having regained his card, he finished in the money 18 times in 24 PGA Tour starts, his best result being a T4 at the FedEx St. Jude Classic. He began 2011 with a T15 in the Transitions Championship and a T9 at The Heritage. He's become one of the Tour's most accurate drivers. In 2010 he hit 70.44% of his fairways and ranked 14th.

"I just want to play good golf," Garrett says. "I just want to be able to play the golf that I know I'm capable of playing."

CASE STUDY 107-03

Name: Nancy Lopez

Occupation: LPGA Tour professional   **Age:** 54

LPGA Tour Driving Average (2004): 248.1 yards

LPGA Tour Driving Accuracy (2004): 48.7%

Putts Per Round (2004): 31.36

Self-Evaluation (2011): "When I played in tournaments, I got up early. I went to the golf course early to sign autographs, because fans would catch me as I got out of my car. I had to pace myself, because I wasn't going to NOT sign an autograph. It was a timing issue. If I was rushed, my tempo was off. I always had to keep it slow, nothing quick. It was really a big deal."

Analyst: John Novosel Sr.

Training Site: N/A

Diagnosis: Lopez, winner of 48 LPGA tournaments and a member of the LPGA and World Golf Halls of Fame, has never been a client. I keep a file on her because her tempo history is one of the most unusual of any tour player we've studied. I first timed Nancy in 2003, when she was raising three children and playing no more than a dozen events a year. Her tempo was a hard-to-believe 50/10. *Five-to-one!* (A record for any tour.) *Two whole seconds from takeaway to impact!* (Also a record.) Figuring that motherhood, middle-age and possibly arthritis accounted for her creaky takeaway, I downloaded video of Nancy's swing from the 1980s, when she was less dominant but still winning several tournaments per year. Same thing. She started her takeaway with an "upward press"—not a forward press, but a lifting or uncocking of her hands and arms above the ball—followed by a way-inside backswing, a quick re-cocking of the wrists, a closed clubface, and admirably high hands at the top.

The term "outliers" was not yet in wide circulation, but Lopez's numbers were so far out as to undermine the very premise of Tour Tempo. She was not simply an exception that proved the rule. She was an argument that tempo was *irrelevant.*

Then, for reasons I can't explain, I searched the archives for video of Lopez when she was an LPGA rookie. That, of course, took me back to 1978, when Nancy won nine tournaments, ran away with the rookie-of-the-year and player-of-the-year awards, landed on the cover of *Sports Illustrated,* and captured the hearts of millions of sports fans. Her rookie swing looked very different to my eye, but I didn't realize how different until I powered up the editor and counted her frames. Nancy Lopez, at age 21, was a 30/10.

Classic, unequivocal, accept-no-imitations *Tour Tempo!*

At the beginning of her career, in other words—when she was winning an unprecedented 17 LPGA events in two seasons—Lopez swung her club to the same 3-to-1 rhythm as Sam Snead, Ben Hogan, Arnold Palmer, Gene Littler, and Jack Nicklaus. She then abruptly and dramatically slowed down her swing—did no one notice?—and played another couple of decades as a mere mortal, winning from one to three tournaments per year.

Was Nancy still great? Yes, she was. But she won two-thirds of her career titles with a pokey, lift-the-club-and-pause action that put a governor on her considerable power. It's my opinion that if she had kept swinging at Tour Tempo, she would have definitely surpassed Kathy Whitworth's tour-pro record of 88 wins.

Follow-Up: Lopez, 54, has played very few tournament rounds in recent years. As a three-time former champion, she entered the 2007 and 2010 LPGA Championships, missing the cut on both occasions. But she is always a welcome entrant on the Legends Tour and played for the U.S. team in the 2011 Handa Cup.

"Once I wasn't playing as much, I had to figure out how I could compete," Lopez told John Garrity in a recent interview. When asked if she was aware of how drastically her swing had slowed over the years, she said, "I'm not really sure about that, but now I definitely have to speed up a little. I need some clubhead speed to hit the ball farther."

A faster tempo would, indeed, restore some pop to Nancy's game. Less certain is her aging body's ability to exploit an upgrade to 24/8 or 21/7. "My body hurts more than it used to," she told John. "I have really bad feet—hammertoes—and my knees are very bad, the pain goes up to my hips. I can play and play well, but I really feel it afterwards. And I don't like to take medications." John Jr. would undoubtedly put Lopez on a golf-specific stretching and strength program while speeding up her tempo by stages, starting with our 27/9 tones.

Working on her own, Lopez has cut some frames off her swing, but it's still a meandering 38/10.

One part of Lopez's game is still as sharp as ever: her desire to compete. She said that an LPGA comeback was not out of the question if she could get her body and swing back in shape. She said, "I would give anything if I could walk those fairways again and just compete, maybe finish in the Top 20 two or three times a year. That would be very good."

Assuming her medical issues are treatable, I see no reason why Lopez can't achieve her modest goals. She just needs to recapture the 3-to-1 tempo that made her a world beater three decades ago.

CASE STUDY 27-10

Name: Ron Gring

Occupation: *GOLF Magazine* Top 100 Teaching Professional

Average Driving Distance: N/A

Driving Accuracy: N/A

Putts Per Round: N/A

Self-Analysis (2011): "I'm from L.A.—that's Lower Alabama—and I run Gring Golf at the Magnolia Grove Golf Course on the Robert Trent Jones Golf Trail. I've got a golf doctorate (a Ph.D. in *The Golfing Machine*), I'm a TPI-certified golf trainer, and I coach a number of PGA Tour, Nationwide Tour, Champions Tour and LPGA Tour professionals, including Kenny Perry, Brad Faxon, Joe Durant and Jerry Pate, not to mention hundreds of amateurs."

Analyst: John Novosel Jr.

Training Facility: Titleist Performance Institute, Oceanside, Calif.

Diagnosis: Ron's got a real Southern accent. He's also got one of the better golf swings you've ever seen. He was such a great ball striker that he once went a couple of weeks on tour without missing a fairway or a green.

Ron was coaching Kenny Perry at the 2008 Ryder Cup in Louisville, Ky., when he saw Padraig Harrington warming up with our SpeedBall. (Padraig was "Happy Gilmoring" the impact target, a run-up golf swing being one of his many talents.) That got Ron interested in Tour Tempo, so we set up a meeting at TPI's California facility. He started hitting balls on the range, and just eyeballing his swing, I figured he was no more than 24/8, maybe 21/7.

So I put him on the 21/7 tones, and he started hitting it real bad. I mean, *bad!* Way off line and weak. I said, "That's okay, you're not doing it right." I switched him to the 24/8 tones. Result: More bad shots.

He said, "This is *way* too fast."

"Can't be," I said. "There's no way you're slower than this."

But the tones weren't working, so I put him on 27/9. And I really wish I had video of this, the way he reacted to the 27/9. Ron started hitting it as good as I've ever seen anybody hit a golf ball. He was using 27/9, but I guarantee you, he was swinging 21/7—and crushing it.

So one lesson to be learned is that if you try Tour Tempo and the first few shots are duds, don't get discouraged. Ron is a great player, and his first attempts made him look like a hack. He just wasn't used to someone going *"Swing!—Set! Through!"* Once he got it down, he really loved it.

The second lesson is a rare one. Here's this guy in great physical shape, great golf swing, former tour player, a Top 100 teacher ... and he gets his best results swinging to a much slower 3-to-1 tone. It has everything to do with the way he reacts to the tones.

Follow-Up: Ron and I have become good friends, and I pick his Ph.D. brain when I have technical questions. Ron came up with a modified step drill that we call the "Ron Gring Drill." At the 2011 PGA Merchandise Show, Ron's wife Yvette was nice enough to sit through a "business lunch" while Ron and I exchanged ideas about the golf swing and tempo.

Chapter 17

Pro Tempo FAQs

How do you explain the fact that Tour swings have sped up since 2004?

Has to be *Tour Tempo*, right? When Dad and John were writing the book, I think Jesper Parnevik and Chad Campbell were the only top-ranked pros swinging faster than 21/7. But now you've got Matteo Manassero, Rickie Fowler, Rory McIlroy, Alviro Quiros, a whole bunch of young guys who swing around 18/6. What's more, most of the older pros have juiced up their tempos, cutting three or four frames off their elapsed times to get to 24/8 or 21/7.

Tour Tempo is the only reasonable explanation for the change. The book came out, and the pros learned that it was better to have a fast swing with perfect tempo than a slow swing with perfect tempo.

Because you hit it longer and straighter.

Tour Tempo was a license to speed up. It still is, as long as you honor the 3-to-1 ratio, maintain your spine angle and swing into a balanced follow-through. (Jr.)

I love Fred Couples and his slow, effortless swing. Fred says his only tempo thought is "smooooth." What's wrong with that?

Nothing. What's wrong is your description of Fred's swing as slow and effortless. His 24/8 swing is slightly faster or the same as the swings of Greg

Norman, John Daly, Vijay Singh, and Jim Furyk, and if you raced your swing against his, Fred would probably beat you to the ball by five or ten frames.

Couples means well when he tells amateurs to keep it "slow and smooth," but what feels slow to him is way faster than most amateurs swing.

Same thing with Ernie Els. The TV announcers can't get over how "languid" his swing is. Well, maybe it is—if your definition of languid is .0333 seconds slower on the forward swing. Truth is, Els is only one frame slower than your garden-variety, 24/8 tour pro. (Jr.)

————

Hand Couples a putter, and it's a different story. A few years ago, before he joined the Champions Tour, Fred was one of the worst putters on the planet. He really rushed his forward stroke, absolutely yipped it. Even in his prime, Freddy was a jabber on the greens. Anybody remember how many short putts he missed in the final round of the 1990 PGA Championship at Shoal Creek? It was painful to watch.

Fred's stroke looks a lot better now, so he must have figured it out. Or maybe he started using the iPod loaded with short-game tones that we sent his agent a couple of years back. (JN)

Your fastest putting tones are 14/7. Is there a tour player with a faster rhythm than that?

Yep. Tommy "Two Gloves" Gainey is a 12/6, which means he dispatches his putts in a mere .59 seconds. He must be really eager to get to the next tee, where he can pound out a drive with that unorthodox, Arnold Palmer-like follow-through.

We don't teach Tommy's tempo. We'll add 12/6 to our Total Game app when hummingbirds start playing golf. (JN)

Are there tour players who win tournaments with off-label tempo?

There most definitely are … if by "off-label" you mean something other than the 3-to-1 rhythm used by most tour pros. Kenny Perry has won 14 PGA Tour events and finished second in two majors with a backswing as long as a Cialis commercial. (Perry is 31/8 with his driver; he'd be a 25/8 if he didn't waste 6 frames in transition.) And now we have Mark Wilson, who won two recent tournaments with a 24/6 action. Wilson's not slow, he's fast—thirty frames, total. But, like Perry, he's 4-to-1, which is way off tour tempo.

How do they get away with those tempos? We dunno. It's a topic for future research. But for the best results, we think you should go with what the majority of tour players use—Tour Tempo. (JN)

If Tour Tempo is so important, how do the slower-swinging gals manage to win on the LPGA Tour?

Before I answer, I must remind you that, historically, many of the great women golfers *have* swung to the 3-to-1 standard. Mickey Wright was a brisk 3-to-1. Annika Sorenstam was an even faster 3-to-1. That's 154 LPGA victories right there, including 23 majors. And now we have young Yani Tseng from Taiwan, who has won five majors at the age of 22 with a powerful and repeatable 25/7 rhythm. You wanna' beat Yani? You'd better bring your 3-to-1 swing.

But it's true, LPGA players deviate from Tour Tempo more than their male counterparts do—especially the Asian players, like Japan's Ai Miyazato. "Low and slow" must be a mantra in Japan, because those Japanese girls have super-long, very slow swings. I think they swing that way because they're hyper-mobile and because their coaches are mired in the old paradigm. But don't quote me as criticizing Asian coaches—not while their players are kicking butt on six continents!

How do these gals win with slow-motion swings? I think it's because LPGA course setups aren't stretched to the max. The average yardage for an LPGA Tour golf course is between 6,200 and 6,400 yards. And that's not a bad thing. It gives equal weight to all the golfing skills, rewards good course management, and prevents domination by the long-hitting, Laura Davies-style players.

The PGA Tour, on the other hand, loves the long ball. Its courses average close to 7,400 yards, and most of those yards are lined with significant rough and fairway bunkers that gobble up 285-yard drives. That's why the Tour's shorter hitters look forward to the Pebble Beach National Pro-Am (three courses under 7,000 yards) and The Heritage at Harbour Town Golf Links (6,973 yards). Those setups give the control players a better shot at victory.

That said, I don't expect the women's slow-swing paradigm to continue. As the tempo discoveries of the past decade work their way into the various golf development programs, you'll see the world's coaches crack the whip. They'll get their gals up to speed. (Jr.)

———

Newsflash! You can expect the women's slow-swing paradigm to end fairly soon.

Here's why. When I put the tempo meter on the gals playing in the 2011 NW Arkansas Championship, I observed that the winner, fast-swinging Yani Tseng, led the tour in driving distance. Furthermore, the leaders in driving distance tended to have full swing tempos like those of their PGA Tour counterparts.*

1. Yani Tseng 268	14. Amy Yang 260
2. Maria Hjorth 267	15. Suzann Pettersen 260
3. Michelle Wie 266	17. Belen Mozo 259
4. Brittany Lincicome 266	22. Se Ri Pak 258
6. Ryan O'Toole 265	23. Stacy Lewis 258

Excellent golfers without PGA Tour-type tempos—like #97 Julie Inkster (245 yards) and #94 Ai Miyazato (246 yards)—are giving up over 20 yards to Yani and are probably hitting 5-irons into greens when Yani is using an 8-iron.

And, whoa, this just in! Sixteen-year-old Lexi Thompson has just won the 2011 Navistar Classic, making her the youngest winner in LPGA history. Lexi is long—she averages better than 280 yards per drive—and she's a poster girl for Tour Tempo, timing out at 24/7 with the driver and 21/7 with her irons. A year ago, *The New York Times* reported that she was "wearing a golf glove with the word Tempo written in her girlish scrawl. It is there to remind her not to be in such a rush, to take her time with her swing." (My kind of golfer!)

It's a good thing Lexi has the glove to remind her to slow down, because her tempo, at sixteen, is about the same as Ben Hogan in his prime (and faster than Tiger Woods was when he won the 2002 U.S. Open at Bethpage Black).

Did I mention that she's long? Paired with Meena Lee and Tiffany Joh in the final round, Lexi banged her drives a good 50 yards past her rivals. The night

*I don't have tempo times on every one of the top 25; I have listed only those players whose tempos I have clocked.

before, it was reported, Joh had tweeted her as follows: "Alexis Thompson just don't laugh at me as you walk 120 yards past my ball tomorrow, k? Thanks."

As Bob Dylan said, "The times, they are a-changin." (JN)

Do the pros have their tempo when they get to the course, or do they find it on the range?

Pro tempos are pretty ingrained; those guys don't have to go looking for 3-to-1. Even so, most pros use their pre-round range time to get loose and to reestablish the feel they're looking for. I was amazed, at a Nationwide event in Omaha a couple of years ago, to see Garrett Willis skip his warm-up entirely. Well, he did warm up, but not in the traditional way. He got to the course twenty minutes before his tee time, warmed up in the parking lot with his SpeedBall and Micro Player, and walked straight to the first tee. He striped one down the middle, no problem, and went on to have a fine round.

Lesson: You don't have to beat balls to get warmed up. You just need your body loosened up, and you need to recreate a feel. (Jr.)

Chapter 18

John Novosel Jr.'s Little Red Book

Dear Reader: There are two John Novosels at Tour Tempo. My dad, John Novosel Sr., is the co-author of the Tour Tempo books, and the inventor of the Tour Tempo training tools. I am the Tour Tempo tour rep and Director of Instruction.

It can get confusing. When Dad makes presentations at clinics or golf shows, people can't match him up to the golfer on the book jacket, who is younger, better looking, and left-handed. Meanwhile, I cruise the range at a PGA Tour event, and somebody asks me to autograph the book—which I didn't write!

We're both teachers, but we go about it differently. Dad is a great inventor and has a great mind, and he'd like to implant a Tour Tempo chip in the brain of every last golfer in the world.

Dad's explanation is that he's a very right-brained person—creative, intuitive, able to think outside the box. He claims that I'm very left-brained—logical, literal-minded, organized—and it's pretty much true. You ask my dad how Tour Tempo works, and he'll say, "It's the way most human beings learn to make an athletic, right-brained movement — by reacting to a stimulus. It gets your mind off the old-fashioned 20-point checklist." That's a great answer for the weekend golfer who can't take the club back because he's trying to remember whether Ben Hogan said to "pronate" or "supinate" on the backswing.

You ask me how Tour Tempo works, and I'll pull down an anatomical chart and start explaining the difference between flexion and extension.

Tour players, by and large, are right-brained types like my dad (kinetic, competitive, artistic, independent, impulsive), but they toil in a left-brained workplace (constrained, disciplined, traditional, legalistic, hierarchical). Tour pros are open to new ideas, but only if you can demonstrate that your ideas are supported by theory and proven in application. Luckily, we can do both.

I'm generalizing. Practically speaking, I think you give both the average player and the tour player as little theory as you can—because the more you intellectualize the golf swing, the faster it goes to hell.

Anyway, that's why I'm the tour rep.

Tempo: A Puzzle for Your Brain

Tour Tempo is the kind of discovery that makes you slap your forehead. Why didn't I see that? How could something so obvious go unnoticed for decades?

The answer, of course, is that conventional thinking was stuck with the idea that everybody had their own unique, unchangeable tempo.

A few researchers came close. I was in a club fitter's office one day, around the time the book came out, when I noticed a poster on the wall. Somebody had used stop-action video of a pro's swing to analyze his tempo, and they had timed all the pertinent parts—backswing, forward swing, follow-through. The data was accurate, but it was measured in *hundredths of a seconds.* So if you were to have logged a tempo ratio, it would have looked like this: .79/.27. If you had taken the further step of carrying out the division, you would have gotten 2.9259259—which is pretty darn close to three.

Nobody created that tempo ratio and nobody performed the arithmetic for the simplest of reasons: *They didn't see the 3-to-1 ratio.* It was camouflaged by the unit of measurement.

Dad spotted it because the clock on his video-editing software included a frame counter. When he decided to time Jan Stephenson's backswing and forward swing—don't ask why!—he got two easily-digestible whole numbers: 27 and 9. When he performed the same exercise on a televised Tiger

Woods swing, he got the same result: 27/9. When he timed Jack Nicklaus, he got different numbers—21 and 7—but the reduced fraction was the same: 3-to-1! It was truly a Eureka moment, and it would never have happened without the frame counter.

Frames have proved to be even more important in *teaching* tempo. They provide an easily understood lingo for swing coaches and students, who know exactly what to do when a pupil says, "I'm a 24/8, but lately I'm a couple of frames long at the top." I can't imagine the same conversation expressed in elapsed seconds.

Anyway, I stared at that poster and thought, *Man, if you'd only known what you were looking for.*

A Rising Star

I was hitting my peak in long drive when I first met Gary Woodland. He was a junior at the University of Kansas, and I was interested in him because I saw him as a long-hitting rival and because I wanted to learn more about clubhead speed. Gary's legend was already starting to grow in our part of the world. He was the Topeka kid who went to Washburn University on a basketball scholarship before transferring to Kansas to play golf.

Anyway, I did a fitness-training thing with the KU golf team, and one element of the program was the SpeedBall test, where we asked the kids to whack an impact target with the SpeedBall driver. Gary practically destroyed the target; he busted out a mid-130s mph clubhead speed with his first swing.

Gary is special in that he truly has effortless power. Yeah, I know, everybody says that about tour pros. But if you watch Tiger or J. B. Holmes or Dustin Johnson, you can see that they're really going after it. The effort is visible. With Gary, you watch him hit the drive and you think, "Okay, that was a controlled swing, good balance, and let's see, his ball speed is one hundred and— *eighty eight?* What the hell?"

He's just in his mid-twenties and only a couple of seasons into his PGA Tour career, so Gary's game is still in the formative stage. As he gets better, I expect Gary's tempo to evolve the way Tiger's did in the late '90s. Gary's currently in the 25–26/8–7 range, but his swing will probably shorten to around 22/7 in the next few years. (Gary made the cut in all four majors in 2011. He was

24th at the Masters, 23rd at the U.S. Open, 30th at the British Open and 12th at the PGA Championship. And, of course, won his first PGA Tournament, the 2011 Transitions Championship.)

Debunking the 'Pause at the Top'

When I lecture on tempo, I use the example of my three-year-old daughter learning to jump. She practically plants her bottom on the floor, but she can't jump very well from that position. It will take her awhile to find the right amount of knee flex.

The same laws apply to the adult jumper. When you crouch and leap, your quads and glutes *streeeeetch* ... and then they shorten. But the height of your jump is not determined solely by the strength of those muscles. Time is also a factor.

The Yale professors, in their tempo study, liken it to a harmonic oscillator, which is basically a spring. I express it as how your muscles cycle in elapsed time, because the speed of the stretch-and-shorten sequence is critical. The more powerful jump, any basketball coach will tell you, is the quick crouch and leap. Nobody out-rebounds Dwight Howard by "pausing at the bottom."

The stretch-and-shorten cycle applies to the golf swing, as well. That makes it a myth-buster—the myth being Tommy Armour's notion, spread by his best-selling golf instructionals, that a "pause at the top of the backswing" results in a more rhythmic, more powerful strike. The pause at the top was an article of faith for my dad, for John Garrity's dad, and for practically every amateur of the post-World War II generation. And that explains, if I can say so without offending, why none of them could hit it out of their shadows.

The first tangible benefit of Dad's discovery of Tour Tempo was that he instantly picked up twenty yards of carry with his driver. He rightly credited his improved tempo, which gave him the newfound ability to exploit the stretch-and-shorten cycle and gain those extra yards.

If you're skeptical, check out the swing of Jamie Sadlowski, the long-drive champion. Jamie's got a 19-frame backswing! That's all the time it takes him to get his club past parallel, and then WHAM!, it's six frames down to impact. There is *no*, I repeat, no pause at the top. And Jamie's ball—if it doesn't shatter, it rockets out there about 380 yards before landing.

Letting Lefty Be Lefty

Phil Mickelson is a very interesting case. In *Tour Tempo,* Dad used Phil as an example of a great player whose shot quality could often be judged by the frame counts of his videos. Phil would hit driver off the deck on his way to eagling a 650-yard par 5, and Dad would time him at a perfect 27/9. A week later, Phil would hook his 3-wood into a bayou, and Dad would clock him at a lurchy 30/8. Phil's bad shots were as easy to diagnose as a case of measles. You could see the wasted frames at the top of his backswing—his hands would move laterally an inch or so, or he'd maneuver the club shaft to get it back on plane.

Fortunately for Phil, his full-swing tempo is on more weeks than it is off. Forty-odd pro wins, four majors, and an estimated $50 million annual income testify to that.

It wasn't until we discovered the 2-to-1 short-game tempo that we realized how unusual Lefty is. The best players hole their putts and hit their crisp chips to a fairly consistent 18/9 or 16/8, give or take a couple of frames, but Mickelson will chip in from the fringe with a 15/7 stroke, hole a long putt with a 19/7, and then rattle a bunker shot off the pin with a 16/6 swipe. By way of contrast, Tiger Woods—the only top player with a short game as good or better than Phil's—used to be a steady 16/8 around the greens.

Phil's inconsistency seemed to catch up with him in the summer of 2008. "He's coming down too fast," Dad said, analyzing a 16/6 Mickelson pitch on his computer. "It's the amateur move, trying to help the ball into the air with the hands and arms." Dad said that with a smile—his way of pointing out that star golfers get the yips, just like the rest of us.

Anyway, we got a call from Mickelson's camp a few weeks later. Eager to help, I sent Phil a Micro Player. (See Chapter 16, "Case Studies.") I subsequently studied a lot of his video, and after watching him putt, chip, blast, pitch and lob in tournament settings, I was beyond impressed. Phil's touch was awesome, his technique was brilliant, and his creativity was incomparable. But I also saw why he threw off inconsistent tempos. It's because he's got about a dozen ways to hit any given shot.

Thirty foot chip shot? How would you like that? Pinched? Cut? Lobbed? Face open? Face closed? Bellied with a wedge? Heeled with a hybrid? Toed with a putter? Left-handed? Right-handed? Spinning left? Spinning right? Checking up? Rolling out? Stopping at the QuikTrip for milk? You name it, Phil's got it.

It reminded me of John Garrity's dad, who was always practicing "swing 25-B" or "swing 17-C." But unlike Mr. Garrity's swings, Phil's don't all look the same. Phil's shots utilize different tempos, depending upon the lie and how much green he has to work with.

The following spring, Phil won his third Masters. His short game was fabulous, and we didn't get a post-tournament call for help.

Looping for Garrett

A television close-up of a tour player gives you some idea of the pressure the pros feel in the heat of competition. You see the furrowed brow, the intense concentration on the yardage book, the curt exchanges with the caddie about club selection or wind direction. But you don't fully grasp their intensity until you're out there with them under the gun—that is, until you caddie for one of them.

I learned that when I caddied for Garrett Willis in the 2010 Midwest Classic in Overland Park, Ks. Garrett is a very nice guy and a good friend, but in competition he is—how can I say it?—*intense.* As his caddie, I experienced that intensity firsthand. (Before he posts a critique of my caddying skills at "pgatour.com," let me point out that he *did* make the cut with me on the bag. I made one good wind call and read one putt for him. Which isn't bad.)

But intensity under pressure is a double-edged sword. Pressure tends to destroy tempo, not to mention your ability to reason, focus, and communicate. That's why it's so important to have your tempo grooved. If your "tempo shield" is impenetrable, you'll have a huge advantage on the field.

Sugar and Spice

My wife is athletic—she's played soccer and other field sports—but she's not a natural golfer. Her backswing is real slow, and her forward swing has no pop. There's no hit.

I see this a lot with my women students. Tempo is not gender-based, but it's my observation that women aren't raised to hit things. Little boys grow up playing baseball, basketball and football; they like to hit, and they like to hit hard. I'm stereotyping here, but little girls grow up doing dance and gymnastics. My daughter loves to swim.

I think this is a huge reason for women golfers' slow tempos. When you learn to hit something hard (little boys), you learn to load the spring; when you learn to load the spring, you gravitate toward the 3-to-1 tempo ratio. When you *don't* hit hard (little girls), you don't load the spring; you don't discover Tour Tempo. Mix in hypermobility and the "cult of slow" in coaching, and *voilà*—you've got slow tempos.

But don't tell that to Yani Tseng. At the time of this writing, Yani is the world's top-ranked woman golfer and the youngest player, male or female, to win five major championships. Yani's driving average is better than 268 yards and her tempo is a dynamic 25/7.

She can hit.

Who is Golf's Power King?

Tour Tempo was really rolling when I started to get into long-drive. I wanted to see how the longest hitters in the world fit into the tempo scheme, so I started timing golf's dedicated ball-bashers, the big boys of long drive. Guys like Jason Eslinger, who is 6′1″ and 240 pounds. (He is a 21/7. Fast.)

And then I got hold of a video of two-time RE/MAX World Long Drive champion Jamie Sadlowski.

Whoa.

Pound for pound, Jamie must be the most powerful golfer of all time. Yes, I said MOST POWERFUL, pound for pound, of any golfer who's ever teed it up. Jamie weighs only 165 pounds, but he generates more than 220 miles per hour of ball speed.

To express this idea, I developed a new swing stat—let's call it the "JNJr. ratio"—that compares ball speed to body weight. Jamie's ball speed-to-weight ratio is 220/165, or 1.33. Contrast that with Tiger Woods, who at the height of his powers weighed about 185 pounds and achieved a ball speed of 185 mph. Tiger's ratio was 1.0. I've since rendered this stat for most of the game's long hitters, and believe me, Jamie is truly in a league of his own.*

Jamie's tempo? It's fast. No, it's *greased lightning* fast. It's around 19/6.

You're thinking, *Yeah, 19/6 is pretty fast. But he's no faster than Alviro Quiros, Matteo Manassero, or a dozen other tour pros. What makes Sadlowski so special?*

This: He takes the club back almost to perpendicular.

Not *parallel*—this is *way* past parallel—but *perpendicular.* Jamie's clubhead dips to his belt line. If his clubshaft were a rifle barrel, it would be aimed at the Goodyear blimp.

Jamie's taking the club back about 30% farther than most quick-paced PGA Tour pros, yet he's returning his clubhead to the ball in two to four fewer frames. He goes much farther *both* ways and does it in *less* time. That combination of incredibly fast tempo and an incredibly long swing produces incredibly fast swing speeds. Jamie's clubhead speed with the driver is 140 mph. That's 20 mph faster than the longest tour pros.

Currently, Jamie supplements his long-drive income with "power shows," crowd-pleasing exhibitions that demand the fastest swings he can muster. But he hangs out in Arizona with a lot of PGA Tour players, leading to speculation that he might someday trim a little off his turn and try his hand at tournament golf. If he does, two things are for sure. (1) Jamie Sadlowski will be the longest

---

*When I competed in Long Drive, I was 195/165. My "JNJr. ratio" was 1.18.

hitter on tour and (2), all the other tour players will be standing behind him on the range, gawking.

Preview Chapter from the Soon-to-Arrive Book by John Novosel Jr.

• The Force •

Feel the Force, Luke, Feel the Force.

No, I'm not Obi-Wan-Kenobi, but that's the advice I'd give to both Luke Donald and you. "The Force" is my name for a new way to practice that is based on Tour Tempo and Yale professor Bob Grober's paper titled "Towards a Biomechanical Understanding of Tempo in the Golf Swing."

My dad found the Yale study on the internet. Professor Grober, working with biomedical engineering professor Jacek Cholewicki, had conducted an independent study verifying *Tour Tempo's* main premise (the 3-to-1 backswing-to-forward-swing elapsed-time ratio) and offering a scientific model for the mechanical forces involved. Dad was so excited that he immediately called Yale and got permission to post the paper on our website.

Bob, it turned out, was a golf enthusiast who just happened to be one of the world's top applied physicists. For that reason—and because he has published two subsequent papers on putting mechanics that support our thesis that tournament pros employ a 2-to-1 tempo ratio for their short shots—Bob is my go-to guy when I've got questions on the science of tempo.

Not long ago, for example, I had to prepare a Tour Tempo presentation for the 2011 PGA of Holland Teaching Summit. I started with a basic outline from my 2008 lectures to the PGA of Sweden and the World Golf Fitness Summit, but I like to spice up my presentations with fresh data and the latest discoveries. Going over my notes, I remembered something that Bob had told me—how if you pictured the golfer's body as a spring, that spring would coil and recoil in a 3:1 time ratio … or something like that. Wanting to get it right, I fired off an e-mail to Bob.

He wrote me back: *Relevant to your question, if you imagine the body as a giant spring … wind it up (backswing) by applying a constant force, F1, and then unwind it (downswing) with a force of different magnitude, F2, and in the opposite direction, and if F2 is twice the magnitude of F1 (i.e. you push down twice as hard as you push back), then the ratio will be 3:1. As F2 gets larger than twice F1, then the ratio will get larger.*

We traded a few more e-mails, and he sent me links to his new papers on putting. They both confirmed the 2:1 tempo ratio, and to achieve it you had to use the SAME force on the backswing and downswing. F2 had to equal F1.

Talk about counter-intuitive! If your tempo is a 2-to-1 ratio, you'd assume that your downswing would require two times more force than your backswing. Similarly, you'd associate a long-game tempo ratio of 3-to-1 with a force profile that is also 3-to-1.

But that is NOT the way it is.

As a competitive long-driver, I had always assumed that my downswing required three or four times more force than my backswing. In that respect, I was like my mid- to high-handicap students, who think they have to throw everything they have at the ball on the downswing.

No. Your downswing needs only twice as much force as the backswing.

————

We recognize that a second swing ratio is confusing—particularly when the backswing is the numerator in the tempo fraction and the denominator in the force fraction. That's why we use the term "force profile." When we say "tempo fraction" or "tempo ratio," we're talking about the well-established Tour Tempo metric, which is expressed as whole numbers

(3-to-1) or as frames of video (21/7, 24/8, etc.). When we use the term "force profile," we're referring to the Grober/Cholewicki force fraction (F1-to-F2, 1•1, 1•2), in which F1, the backswing force, has no assigned value. The force profile will be expressed with a circle between the two numbers, like 1•1, for example.

Turning the idea around, one way to create a 3-to-1 Tour Tempo is to feel that you are swinging down with twice the force that you used to swing the club back, namely 1•2.

The same paradigm applies with the short game. To create the 2-to-1 tempo ratio, you need a 1•1 force profile; you use the exact same amount of force to take the club back and through. I repeat, the force of the downswing should match the force of the backswing.

Your putting backswing does not require much force, does it? It's the same for chipping. The principal reason golfers 'flip' when chipping is that they are trying to add force that they don't need.

What I loved about Bob's force profile was its simplicity. I was pretty sure I could apply "The Force" to my own swing, and I thought the average golfer could understand it, as well.

But first I had to take it out of the lab and onto the golf course.

————

Putting was the obvious place to start. Dropping a few balls on the putting green at Alvamar, I let go of all my thoughts about path, release, wrist position, etc. I simply tried to match the force of my forward swing to the force of my backswing.

The results were immediate. I holed putts. My distance control was phenomenal. Best of all, my "swing thought" was more of an awareness, more of a *feel*. I was focused on feeling the forces.

I videotaped my stroke, and guess what? The 1•1 force profile was producing the 2-to-1 tempo!

Chipping was next, and I got the same results. All I had to do to ensure solid contact and a predictable rollout was match F2 to F1. And the point I want to stress is that I needed very little force on the forward swing to match the force of my takeaway.

I pictured the weekend golfer with his greenside flubs and skulls, and it suddenly hit me. The 1•1 force profile was to the chipping yips what the gum eraser was to badly-drawn lines.

It made them disappear.

———

I discussed Bob Grober's force hypothesis with John Sr., who suggested we meet at Hallbrook to study it further. Dad's method is all about feel, so "feel the force" was right in his wheelhouse. He played around with the concept before we met, and he found that it was important to use the Tour Tempo short-game tones to establish the feeling of the 1•1 force profile; it established a baseline feel for an equal-force backswing and downswing. He also developed a great drill to use with it.

To start, he had me hit ten 9-iron shots with the 18/9 tones. He then took five balls and lined them up on the range, Charles Barkley style, and had me hit shots with the 1•1 force profile without the tones. Then he lined up five more balls and had me hit them with the 1•2 force profile, again without the tones. The next step was to alternate between the two forces. The results were really solid shots and Tour Tempo tempo. But would it work on the ultimate testing ground? The golf course is where swing theories usually get challenged.

We headed to the first tee. The course was open, so I hit a few drivers, trying to feel the 1•2 force profile. I pounded them long and straight. Again, I felt like I had a swing thought ... but it wasn't so much a thought as a feel. It was a great focus to have.

The lightbulb-over-my-head insight was this: If I wanted a faster downswing, which is an absolute must for long-driving, then I had to add more force to my *backswing*.

I tried it on the next tee, and another solid drive soared down the fairway.

'Feel the Force' Drill

1. Start out with the short-game tones (we like 18/9) and hit about 10 to 15 pitching wedges or 9-irons. (Only use the short-game tones with this part of the drill.)

2. Line up five balls. Using a Y or L drill, brush the grass with some practice swings, feeling the 1•1 force profile. Feel like you're using the SAME amount

of force for your backswing and downswing. Then go ahead and hit the five balls, making sure that F2 equals F1.

3. Line up another five balls. Using more of a full-swing motion, brush the grass with some practice swings, feeling the **1•2** force profile. Use TWICE the amount of force in your downswing that you used in your backswing. Then go ahead and hit the five balls, making sure that F2 equals twice the force of F1.

4. Line up five more balls and alternate between the **1•1** force profile and the **1•2** force profile, feeling the difference between the forces. You can also throw in some chip shots for the **1•1** force when alternating the forces.

When feeling "The Force," your focus should be on the forces you apply to the swing. Don't think about positions, angles, turning, or anything else. Just apply the proper forces.

———

When you use Tour Tempo with the Force Drill, you will develop that most elusive of golf attributes: "awareness." Tour pros don't know how to describe this attribute, but they know they are aware of what they are doing in a way that most amateurs are not. Thanks to their heightened awareness—which observers characterize as "feel"—the pros can control both the timing (tempo) and effort-level (power) of their swings.

You may be left-brained (like me), so go ahead and intellectualize it. Your clubhead travels a relatively short distance when you're putting, chipping or pitching to the 2-to-1 tempo tones, so you don't need more than your takeaway force to swing back down and through the ball. With the 3-to-1 full-swing tones, however, you've got to bring the clubhead further down in less time; so you need more force. *Twice* as much force, to be precise.

It really makes sense, and here's the best part: It's SIMPLE.

The Real World

My dad always says, "If you want to learn how to do a job the best possible way, find out what the pros in that field are doing and what tools they are using to get the job done." This applies doubly to the golf swing. If you want to improve, you should do what the pros do and not what most amateurs do. That sounds kind of Yogi Berra-ish, but there's a lot of truth in it.

To test the idea, let's compare the force profile of the typical tour pro with that of the average golfer. Go to the range at a PGA Tour event and talk to the spectators. They'll tell you that the pros "look like they're swinging so effortlessly." And this baffles the fans because the balls rocketing downrange are clear evidence that the pros are actually swinging quite fast.

But now that you understand force profiles, you know why the pro swings look so effortless. Luke Donald and Keegan Bradley are swinging down with only twice their backswing force, and that doesn't take much effort. On short-backswing shots, they're using the same effort in both directions. Both profiles produce Tour Tempo tempos and tour-quality golf shots.

Now, stroll out to your club's practice range about an hour before the shotgun start of a scramble. You'll see a considerable amount of lunging, heaving, and garden-variety overexertion, but you won't see many balls rocketing down-range. That's because everyone is using way too much downswing force. This produces odd, inconsistent tempos and wild, inconsistent shots.

Why do amateurs swing this way? It's not the most natural or instinctive way to strike or propel something. Asked to drive home a nail, you don't suspend the hammer over the nail head and then push down hard on it. Asked to sneak a fastball past Albert Pujols, you don't throw it flatfooted (see Tim Lincecum). To be effective, these actions require an initiating force applied in the "wrong" direction– a backswing, a wind-up, a coiling—to load the biomechanical spring for the hit, throw, or kick.

We're golfers, so let's just focus on the golf swing. No, on second thought, let's focus on how we *perceive* the golf swing. Let's talk paradigms.

Paradigm A: "It's all about the backswing." This paradigm, which has dominated golf instruction since the days of Bobby Jones, grew out of direct observation and sound reasoning. Conventional teaching acknowledged that the clubhead was moving too fast on the downswing to make any conscious changes to its orientation or path. It followed, therefore, that a quality hit depended upon the golfer getting his body and the club into certain optimal positions before unwinding into the ball.

Paradigm A was compelling—so compelling that many of the game's top teachers still spend much of their range time as amateur chiropractors, yanking on their pupils' shoulders and propping up their chins until the club traces the approved (although often jerky) path to the top. Decades of backswing-centered instruction culminated in the "low and slow" orthodoxy, which held that the golfer's takeaway should be very deliberate, "quickness" being the root of all swing evils.

Paradigm B: "It's all about the impact position." This paradigm goes back a decade or so, and it, too, is based on observation and reasoning. Certain pros, many of them tour players, began to point out the obvious: that the world's best golfers did not necessarily have classic backswings. Jack Nicklaus stuck out his right elbow. Lee Trevino looped the club on an outside-to-inside path. John Daly swung the clubhead back so far that it nearly hit his left hip. But all the top players, you had to agree, looked the same at impact—weight on the leading foot, a flat left wrist, forward shaft lean, etc.

––––––––––

So we've got these two golf paradigms. **A** teaches that the backswing is pretty much the whole ball of wax, and **B** teaches that backswings are more about style and are not fundamental to good ball striking. Most golfers subscribe to either **A** *or* **B** and some to **A** *and* **B**. But now, thanks to modern science, we know exactly what *happens* in a golf swing. We know *where* every body part is *at any millisecond* in the swing. The problem is, you haven't been taught exactly how the swing *feels*.

That could explain why golf is so hard for most people.

Anyway, the point I want to make is this: There's a new golf paradigm, based on Tour Tempo and Bob Grober's biomechanics research, that offers a unified theory of the golf swing. Only now it's not about positions, paths and angles. It's about applied force and timing. It's about "loading and unloading the spring." It's about "feel."

Furthermore, this new approach produces the classic impact position of the pros—weight on the leading foot, flat left wrist, forward shaft lean, etc.— without you having to consciously think about any of the moves.

It's simple, it's quick, and it's supported by the latest golf science.

It's Tour Tempo squared.

I call it THE FORCE.

John Novosel Jr.'s book will be published by Tour Tempo, LLC in 2012. Until then, may 'The Force' be with you!

1st Edition

Photographs by John Garrity, except for Chapter 2, 10, 18, and the preview chapter by Team Novosel. Short-game tones and instructional videos produced by Team Novosel for Tour Tempo, LLC.

THE BAG ROOM

TourTempo.com

JOHN NOVOSEL WITH JOHN GARRITY

TOUR TEMPO

GOLF'S LAST SECRET FINALLY REVEALED

POWER TOOLS®
Motion Mechanics®

"The POWER TOOLS club is an unbelievable way to actually feel how to release the clubhead through impact. I increased more than 20 yards on each iron and over 40 yards on my driver. Feeling where to release was an enormous breakthrough in my game."
—JC, Boston, MA

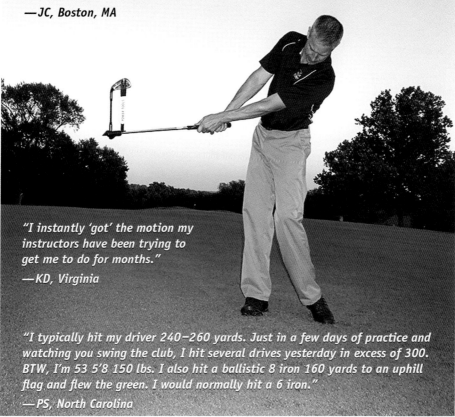

"I instantly 'got' the motion my instructors have been trying to get me to do for months."
—KD, Virginia

"I typically hit my driver 240–260 yards. Just in a few days of practice and watching you swing the club, I hit several drives yesterday in excess of 300. BTW, I'm 53 5'8 150 lbs. I also hit a ballistic 8 iron 160 yards to an uphill flag and flew the green. I would normally hit a 6 iron."
—PS, North Carolina

SpeedBall®

"My problem, like many golfers, was that I came 'over the top' and had a poor impact position (flipping at the ball). By using the SpeedBall, I've been able to correct both these swings faults, plus I have restored my lost distance without thinking about it—and that's what makes the SpeedBall such a great training aid."
—Al Vermeil

Al Vermeil is the only strength coach to have World Championship rings from BOTH the NFL and the NBA.

TOUR TEMPO® VIP

GOLF SCHOOL

"I shot a 66 the Saturday after the school, and then finished the year by winning my club championship." —AC, Memphis

JOHN NOVOSEL'S

TOUR TEMPO®

LONG GAME   SHORT GAME

TONES   VOICE

18/6	21/7	24/8	27/9

 Main   Tracks   Video   Tour Tempo

ALSO BY JOHN GARRITY ....

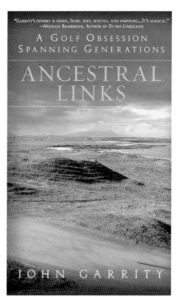

"Every so often a truly beautiful book comes along. This is one of them." *The Irish Times*

"A memoir-travelogue like none other." *Buenos Aires Herald*

"A deeply soulful and personal journey." *Michigan Golf News*

"A gem: a refreshing memoir rife with history, poignance, and good humor." *Sports Illustrated*

"MY FAVORITE OF THE YEAR ... It's a great exploration about family and golf and the way we feel about both. Very, very moving ... an incredible book." *Peter Kessler, XM Satellite Radio*

Published by New American Library

TIGER 2.0: THE BEST GOLF WRITING OF JOHN GARRITY (SPORTS ILLUSTRATED BOOKS)

"*Tiger 2.0* is wonderful—full of fun and charm from beginning to end." *Golf in the Kingdom* author Michael Murphy

"The man is a genius!" CBS golf analyst David Feherty

"*Tiger 2.0* takes the reader on a wonderful, informative, fun-filled golf journey." *Semi-Tough* author Dan Jenkins

"If there was any doubt that Garrity is the best golf writer in the business, this anthology should dispel it." *The Scorecard Always Lies* author Chris Lewis

"The 21 pieces in this collection confirm what Garrity readers voluntarily attest: The *Great* in the subtitle is no hype." *Bernard Darwin on Golf* author Jeff Silverman

Links

TourTempo.eu

TourTempo.com

JohnGarrityOnline.com

JGarrity2.wordpress.com

TourTempo.com/golfstrong

TourTempo.com/yale.pdf

TourTempo.com/multimedia